THE GOURMET
VEGETARIAN SLOW COOKER

❧ THE GOURMET ❧
VEGETARIAN
SLOW COOKER

Simple *and* Sophisticated Meals *from* around *the* World

Lynn Alley

PHOTOGRAPHY BY

Leo Gong

TEN SPEED PRESS
Berkeley

Copyright © 2010 by Lynn Alley
Photographs copyright © 2010 by Leo Gong

Published in the United States by Ten Speed Press, an imprint of the
Crown Publishing Group, a division of Random House, Inc., New York.
www.crownpublishing.com
www.tenspeed.com

Ten Speed Press and the Ten Speed Press colophon are registered
trademarks of Random House, Inc.

Library of Congress Cataloging-in-Publication Data
Alley, Lynn.
  The gourmet vegetarian slow cooker : simple and sophisticated meals
from around the world / Lynn Alley ; photography by Leo Gong. — 1st ed.
      p. cm.
  Includes index.
  Summary: "A vegetarian approach to the slow-cooker phenomenon,
from the author of the best-selling Gourmet Slow Cooker series,
featuring innovative and time-saving meatless recipes from Indian,
Mexican and Southwestern, Asian, Italian, French, Greek, and Middle
Eastern cuisine"—Provided by publisher.
  1. Electric cookery, Slow. 2. Vegetarian cookery. I. Title.
  TX827.A436 2010
  641.5'636—dc22

                          2009034719

ISBN 978-0-307-29225-4

Printed in China

Cover design by Chloe Rawlins based on an original design
by Catherine Jacobes
Text design by Catherine Jacobes
Production by Chloe Rawlins
Food styling by Karen Shinto
Prop styling by Christine Wolheim

10 9 8 7 6 5 4 3 2 1

First Hardcover Edition

To M., as always, with love and gratitude.

CONTENTS

Acknowledgments

Many streams of thought, many recipes, many meals, and many people converge within the pages of a book.

So acknowledging everyone is a daunting thought. Let me start where I can and wend my way along until I've covered those who seem to have played a most important role in the book.

To begin with, let me send warm thank yous out to Aunt Sarah and Aunt Mae, my mother's aunts, who showed me how wonderful vegetables straight from the garden could be. To France, spiritual home to good cooks everywhere, where at one time visitors would be hard-pressed to find a bad meal, and weekly markets were a joy to behold.

To some of the chefs and authors who have inspired me: India-born chefs Neela Paniz and Suvir Saran for their dedication to the cooking of their homeland. To Laurel Robertson for lighting the way and inspiring so many of my generation to kick the meat habit back in the '70s. To Alice Waters for skillfully drawing my attention to the excitement of vegetables. To Deborah Madison for her pioneering role in elevating vegetarian cooking to an art form. To Julia Child for being the light that she was in the world, both personally and professionally.

To my editors at Ten Speed, Melissa Moore and Dawn Yanagihara, for their guidance and hard work. To Phil Wood, now "publisher emeritus" at Ten Speed, for always supporting my manuscripts and encouraging my work. To the very kind Aaron Wehner, who has taken over the helm at Ten Speed, one of the few publishers willing to work well and directly with their authors. To Kristin Casemore, Ten Speed's hardworking cookbook publicist. To Chloe Rawlins, Leo Gong, and Karen Shinto for creating such a lovely book.

On the very practical side, I'd like to thank Valerie Gleason of the EdgeCraft Corporation for making the most wonderful knife sharpener available to the home cook. To Melissa Palmer at the All-Clad Corporation.

To Chibi, Jai, and the many animal friends who have provided unconditional love, warmth, support, friendship, and grounding. They all deserve better than being eaten.

To my dear friend Kathy Fleming, of Accomplishment Coaching, the world's clearest and most astute friend and coach.

To Beth Hensperger, an inspired cook and a hardworking author, who has taught me some invaluable lessons.

To my mom, Margaret Zink, for being a good friend and helper.

Introduction

As I wrote in the introduction to *The Gourmet Slow Cooker*, my first experiments with a slow cooker involved beans.

I was living in a mobile home on a farm in Davis, California, for several months, and the only equipment in the old kitchen was a vintage 1970s slow cooker and a very clunky, battle-scarred frying pan. The drive in to town was more than just the hop down the road I was used to at home, so I tried to buy up at the beginning of the week and keep it really simple.

The solution to the problem seemed to be beans. I went to the Davis Co-op and bought as many different kinds of beans as they had. Each day, I'd put a different kind of bean on to cook in the slow cooker. When the beans were tender, I'd add some good salt and choose an herb or two from the small herb garden outside the double-wide. A dash of olive oil gave my beans a bit of staying power.

And that was how I learned to appreciate the fact that not all beans taste the same. And not all beans have the same color or texture, for that matter.

This was a terrific experiment for me. It enabled me to experience something that country folk throughout the world have long known: how to take what you've got in the back forty and turn it into something that will keep you happy and well nourished.

In Italy, such cooking has been dubbed *la cucina povera*, roughly translated as "the cooking of the poor," or, more graciously, "country cooking." It doesn't entail using exotic and expensive ingredients from around the world. It involves the artful combining and preparing of what is at hand.

Examples abound throughout this book. Think of the simple Cracked Wheat Berries with Honey and Ricotta breakfast, or the Risotto with Lentils from the Italian chapter. Or the French Alpine Cheese, Tomato, and Onion Soup which utilizes summer tomatoes, onions, bread, and cheese from France's alpine regions. Or the Scalloped Potatoes Auvergnats, which calls for potatoes and blue cheese made in the central French region of Auvergne. Or the Baby Limas with Spinach of the Greek chapter. Or the Armenian Apricot Soup, which juxtaposes apricots from the region of their birth with the humble lentil.

Although I am a food and wine writer, and have partaken of many very elegant meals prepared by professional kitchen artists and craftspeople, I admit that some of my favorite meals have been the simplest. Fried okra, just picked from a friend's garden and piping hot on a paper towel. Warm, fresh-picked tomatoes that have never seen the inside of the refrigerator, dusted with a pinch of salt. Bread fresh from a Spanish oven with a cooling gazpacho of tomatoes, cucumbers, and onions.

Those wonderful slow-cooked beans, too, remain in my heart and in my pantry. (Nowadays, I often slow-cook a pot full of beans, salt them, then freeze them in individual portions so that I have something on hand either to eat unembellished or to use as a base for a soup, stew, or salad when the need arises.)

It is my hope that the recipes in this book will honor the traditions of those people who have used what they had in their kitchens, pantries, and gardens in countries around the world.

Some of the dishes (such as the Italian and French recipes) come from cultures where "bare bones basic" works. Some (like the Indian and Mexican recipes) come from cultures that have traditionally drawn upon a more complex mélange of ingredients and cooking techniques.

All the dishes, however, are vegetable-based and reflective of the cultures from which they are drawn, and hence timely for the modern American kitchen, in terms of both health interests and economic considerations, in a world where many of us are realizing that we can live well and happily on a lot less than what we've been conditioned to believe.

Most important, recipes without meat make a statement of compassion for the animals cruelly confined to factory farms throughout the world. Whether or not we consumers choose to see and acknowledge their suffering, it exists and we can choose to be a party to it or not through our food choices.

Cooking Times

You will find this book contains a mélange of dishes inspired by cultures around the world and a variety of cooking times. Some of the dishes require relatively short periods of cooking (2 to 3 hours or so). These dishes have generally been chosen because they highlight something the slow cooker does particularly well, such as taking the tedious stirring out of making risotto or polenta, or baking a successful custard over a longer period of time than is required in the oven. Bread puddings turn out particularly well in a slow cooker. And melting chocolate, like making a fondue, can be done especially well with the gentle, controlled heat provided by a slow cooker.

Other dishes call for a moderate period of cooking, anywhere from 4 to 6 hours. These are dishes that are either based on legumes, like lentils, that do not require extensive cooking, or sturdier vegetables (such as carrots, potatoes, and winter squashes)

that can actually stand up to and be improved by moderate cooking times.

And lastly, there are recipes, generally based on grains or beans, that are at their best when subjected to a nice, long, juicy slow cook.

Unless otherwise stated, all the recipes in this book were tested in a 5-quart slow cooker. (I keep a 3-quart slow cooker for making risotto, polenta, and small amounts of anything, and for melting chocolate, but I do nearly everything else in a 5-quart slow cooker. I also keep two 7-quart slow cookers for entertaining, and a couple of very small ones for when I want to cook for just myself.)

This means that the recipes in the book are calculated to "work" at the specified times in a 5- or 6-quart slow cooker. So the first time you try a recipe from this book, you may want to watch it carefully and adjust your cooking times accordingly, especially if you are using a slow cooker of some other size. The cooking time for a 7-quart slow cooker, for instance, may be significantly shorter than for a 5-quart cooker.

Cooking times may also vary according to manufacturer and price. I am a firm believer in using the relatively cheap slow cookers that I buy at Walmart or Home Depot. They are generally very effective. The only real drawback I have found is that often the heating coils in a cheaper slow cooker may heat less evenly than those in the more expensive models.

This uneven heat source may mean that one side will brown more rapidly than the other. And the only time this makes a real difference is if you are baking a cake, which few people except me do in a slow cooker, or making a custard or bread pudding. (My makeshift solution to the problem has been to use very thick oven mitts to lift and turn the slow cooker insert halfway through the cooking period for a more even cooking. This must be done very carefully, if at all, because the insert is likely to be quite hot.)

The more expensive models also often have digital control panels rather than manual. To me, this means one more thing that could go wrong if the digital panel goes on the fritz. I prefer the manual controls found on most of the cheaper models.

The more expensive models may have more bells and whistles, such as a classy-looking gourmet "finish," or the ability to program the cooker to turn off after a certain number of hours. If this kind of stuff is important to you, then by all means, invest in the bells and whistles.

All-Clad has a lovely, relatively expensive cooker that offers a cast-aluminum insert, rather than the conventional porcelain, that can go straight from the stove top into the slow cooker. This innovation saves on cleanup when you are browning ingredients before slow-cooking them.

And lastly, cooking times may vary in accordance with different types of ingredients. Not all potatoes, for instance, cook at the same rate. New potatoes tend to be waxy and have a firm texture that holds up under longer cooking periods, while tiny white rose potatoes or russets cut into cubes can be cooked in a matter of a couple of hours. "Old" beans take longer to cook than relatively recently harvested beans.

Ingredients and Resources

BEANS

Each type of bean has a unique texture and flavor, many of which I discovered during my first forays with a slow cooker years ago. It's no wonder that some form of bean dish is found in nearly every culture on earth. Beans have provided protein and energy for human health, life, and growth—especially when combined with grains—for thousands of years. And beans were among the first offerings to the gods and goddesses after the harvest.

The liquid left from cooking beans, when not served with them, is a bonus that can enliven soups and other dishes. Large white beans, for instance, leave lots of starch in their cooking broth, making the thick, gelatinous liquid almost perfect for thickening vegetable soups and stews.

Slow-cooked beans taste great, and the long, slow cook often yields an almost creamy product that absorbs the flavors of herbs, spices, fats, and aromatic vegetables added to the pot.

Dried beans should ideally be cooked and eaten within a year of harvest, but most of the time we as consumers have no idea about the condition of our beans. So here are a couple tips for buying beans.

- Look for a store or source that has a rapid turnover of beans. They are more likely to be selling recently harvested beans than stores where the beans have been sitting on the shelf for eons.

- The appearance of the beans can give you some clues as to how long they've been stored. Beans that are split, cracked, or chipped have probably been around for longer than we would like.

Remember that the condition and length of storage of the beans may affect cooking times. Occasionally, I will hear a cook complain about cooking beans for as long as 14 hours, only to find skins that still remain tough and inedible. "Fresh" dried beans will always cook within a reasonable amount of time.

OLIVE OIL

Some olive oil is suitable for cooking, while some is more suitable for what chefs call "finishing" a dish. The less expensive olive oils, usually found in large quantities at a grocery store, are often suitable for cooking purposes. You can use them to brown onions or sauté vegetables. But the more expensive extra virgin olive oils are best when not subjected to the high heat of cooking, and are instead drizzled over a dish or stirred in at the last minute.

SALT

Most of us grew up thinking that salt is salt, but there can be great variations in flavor, texture, and even color depending on where the salt came from, how it was formed, and what's in it.

I rarely use conventional "table salt" in my cooking anymore (with the exception that I still use salt from a box for basic, large-scale cooking needs, such as soups and stews). This is because I have found that the "good" salt called for in my recipes has so much more to offer in terms of flavor and often texture than does good old Morton's. A sprinkling of my favorite gray sea salt, for instance, is often all it takes to elevate a poached egg on toast to something very special.

For this reason, you will find my recipes call for "salt to taste" rather than specific amounts of salt. If you are using conventional table salt, for instance, you should know that it is considered to be twice as potent by volume as kosher or large-grained specialty salt. So let your taste be your guide when it comes to salting your creations.

Most specialty salts are large-grained and require some crushing before you can sprinkle them on your food. To this end, many stores sell special salt mills, which are like pepper mills, only designed for salt. Trouble is, many specialty salts are somewhat moist, and this moisture can gum up the works of a salt mill, even those made for specialty salts. So I have taken to grinding salt crystals by hand in a small Japanese *suribachi* (a sort of Japanese mortar with a ridged inner surface and wooden pestle) purchased at Sur La Table (www.surlatable.com). I have one for grinding salt and one for grinding other spices.

Sea Star Sea Salt is my delicious all-purpose standby. Sea Star (www.seastarseasalt.com) is owned by chef Holly Peterson, who teaches food and wine dynamics at the Culinary Institute of America in Napa Valley. Holly sources her salt from Brittany, where it is farmed in the traditional manner. I have a handmade ceramic seashell that sits on a shelf above my kitchen stove and holds my salt stash. Next to it stands the little *suribachi* for grinding. It takes just a few minutes to smoosh up a batch of salt, but it makes all the difference in the world.

Another "trick" I like to use is adding smoked salt for a smoky flavor to a vegetable dish that might ordinarily get its flavor from a smoked meat such as sausage, ham, or bacon. (See the Smoky Potage Saint-Germain recipe on page 79.)

Playing around with and learning about this basic ingredient is a lot of fun, and although salts are not inexpensive by grocery store standards, a little bit can do a great deal to make an inexpensive meal taste like "the Ritz."

Here are a few sources where you can learn a bit and order salt:

www.napastyle.com

www.saltworks.us

www.salttraders.com

www.seastarseasalt.com

www.atthemeadow.com

SPICES

Although most of the herbs I use come fresh from my garden, spices (usually the seeds or bark of a plant rather than the leaves) are not so easily grown at home. My favorite source for most spices is Penzeys Spices (www.penzeys.com). I order from them online regularly. They source high-quality spices and have a large and rapid turnover offered at reasonable prices. Sit back, thumb through the online catalog, and go shopping right from your armchair!

I should also note that I generally buy spices whole so that I can grind them fresh just before using. Just as freshly ground pepper is more pungent and aromatic than preground pepper that has been sitting on the shelf for who-knows-how-long, spices, too, have more to offer if they are ground just before using. In addition, grinding your own spices means that you have more control over the texture of the finished product. Sometimes I like my spices ground to a fine powder, much like how they would come out of a jar. Other times, I like them to retain some texture, especially in dishes where I want to convey a very "rustic" feel. For this reason, I have both an electric coffee grinder that is used only for spices and a couple of small Japanese *suribachi* that I use for crushing spices. (See further discussion and sources, page 10.)

USEFUL EQUIPMENT

Electric Coffee Mill

An electric coffee mill that is dedicated to grinding spices is a very useful item to have on hand. Instead of buying your spices ground, you will find fresher and more interesting flavors if you buy whole spices and grind them yourself just before using. It takes only a few minutes more, but makes a great deal of difference in your cooking.

Immersion Blender

A handheld immersion blender looks like a long stick with a handle at one end and a tiny metal detector at the other end. It makes life with a slow cooker a breeze. Gone are the days when you have to transfer large batches of stuff by hand from the crock to a blender, blend them, then return them to the pot, leaving soup slopped all over the countertop and your clothes. You just plunge the head of the immersion blender into your beans (or whatever), turn on the blender, and purée your ingredients within minutes. It is important to keep the head of the blender *under* the surface of your food. If the head rises above the surface, stuff will fly everywhere—all over you and your kitchen.

Mortar and Pestle

I have many different sizes of mortars and pestles and have collected them for years. (The most beautiful one I have ever used was in France. It was an antique and belonged to the proprietor of a French farmhouse where I had gone to teach cooking classes. It must have weighed at least 40 pounds and was large enough to make a quart of mayonnaise in. If I thought I could have carried it home on the plane, I would have tried to buy it!) I find them most useful for grinding spices by hand, liberating flavors and aromas while retaining some interesting textures. I strongly recommend that if you really love to cook, you look around for some interesting examples and try them.

India

Spiced Basmati Rice Breakfast Cereal 15

Curried Chickpeas with Fresh Ginger and Cilantro 17

Creamy Dal 18

Dal with Ground Cinnamon, Cloves, Cardamom, and Cumin 19

Stuffed Peppers with Yogurt Sauce 20

Waari Muth 21

Potatoes and Carrots in Coconut Curry 22

Mogul Eggplant 23

Minted Potato and Chickpea Curry 25

Spicy Indian Lentil and Tomato Soup 26

Tomato, Rice, and Coriander Soup 27

What could be more perfect for a book on vegetarian slow cooking than a chapter on India, a country where the majority of people are vegetarian?

In northern India, you may find meat eaters, Muslims and sometimes Sikhs, whose roots and traditions come from the meat-eating cultures to the west of India. This is the home of lamb, beef, and chicken curries. It is interesting to note that in the United States, just as Greek restaurants offer a somewhat limited picture of true Greek cuisine, most "Indian" restaurants are run by immigrants from northern India, often Sikhs, and their culinary traditions include plenty of meat dishes. For the most part, however, the vast majority of Indians are Hindus and do not consume flesh. As a result, the Indian subcontinent is a vegetarian's dream come true in terms of variety, color, and flavor.

Perhaps the most distinguishing hallmark of Indian cuisine is the use of a wide array of spices. Traditionally, each cook mixes her own spices. And traditionally, there is no such thing as "curry powder" among Indian cooks. There are just custom spice blends. (Curry powder is considered to be an invention of the British, who wanted an easy way to approximate the complex flavors found in Indian dishes.)

True, there are characteristic spices that appear over and over again in Indian dishes, but the proportions and specific blends are very much an individual or regional thing. For this reason, most of the dishes in this chapter call for spices to be blended by the cook either in a mortar and pestle or in an electric coffee mill. If you plan to grind spices in a coffee mill, I suggest keeping one mill for your coffee and one just for spices so that the flavors don't mix with one another. You can buy mortars and pestles from any number of different sources, but India-born chef Suvir Saran has designed one specifically to grind Indian spices by hand easily (http://americanmasala.com/collection/main.html).

WINES WITH INDIAN FOOD

India does not have a long-standing tradition of winemaking and wine drinking, probably due to the pervasive Muslim influence in the country. Typically, affluent Indians would offer cocktails before dinner (à la British raj), then drink water or beer with the meal itself. Things are now changing as affluent Indians adopt Western ways, including the taste for wine. There is even a small but growing government-supported wine industry in India.

The complexity of flavors and spices found in Indian cuisine makes it perhaps the most difficult of Asian cuisines for matching with wines. In general, I like aromatic whites such as Gewürztraminer, Riesling, Pinot Blanc and Gris, Müller-Thurgau, Albariño, and Chenin Blanc. Off-dry whites may also work well. Prosecco and other sparkling wines are often great partners for Indian food.

Rosé wines can also work with Indian dishes. Appropriate reds are a bit more difficult to find, and you will want to avoid anything with a lot of tannins, because tannins tend to intensify heat. You'd probably be better off sticking with the lighter, fruitier, younger reds such as French or Oregon Pinot Noir, Grenache, and Beaujolais.

SPICED BASMATI RICE BREAKFAST CEREAL

∾ Serves 4 ∾

Most Americans would consider eating oatmeal for breakfast, but for the vast majority of Asians, rice is the breakfast food of choice. Here is a distinctively Indian variation on the Asian breakfast theme that can be cooked while you sleep and be ready for breakfast when you wake up.

Place the rice and water in the slow cooker insert, cover, and cook on low overnight, about 8 hours.

In the morning, grind the cinnamon, cardamom pods, and nutmeg to a powder in an electric coffee mill or a mortar and pestle.

Add the currants and spices to the rice and stir in 15 minutes before serving.

Divide the rice among 4 cereal bowls and pour $1/2$ cup milk on top of each serving.

Sprinkle each bowl with the toasted coconut and nuts. Drizzle with honey.

SUGGESTED BEVERAGE: A cup of hot spiced chai would be a perfect complement.

$1^1/2$ cups organic brown basmati rice, rinsed well

$3^1/2$ cups water or soymilk

$1^1/2$ sticks cinnamon

2 green cardamom pods

$1/2$ teaspoon nutmeg, freshly grated if possible

$1/2$ cup currants or raisins

2 cups milk, heavy cream, rice milk, or soymilk

3 tablespoons coconut, flaked and toasted

$1/2$ cup walnuts or almonds, coarsely chopped and toasted

Honey, for drizzling (optional)

Curried Chickpeas with Fresh Ginger and Cilantro

~ Serves 6 to 8 ~

As anyone familiar with Indian food knows, chickpeas are one of the most common types of legumes found on Indian tables. In this popular recipe, the spices and fresh ingredients are added at the very end of the cooking time to preserve optimum flavor and freshness. Regulate the heat by the amount of cayenne you use.

Thoroughly rinse the chickpeas and place them in the slow cooker insert along with the water. Cover and cook on low for 6 to 8 hours, until the chickpeas are tender.

In a large sauté pan, brown the onion in the sesame oil until dark brown in color, about 15 minutes.

Combine the cumin seeds, peppercorns, cloves, cardamom, chile powder, ginger, turmeric, garam masala, and cayenne in an electric coffee mill or a mortar and pestle and grind to a coarse powder.

Add the coarsely ground spices to the onion and continue to cook for another 5 minutes, then add the onion and spices to the cooked chickpeas. Recover and continue cooking for another 30 to 60 minutes.

Using a handheld immersion blender, purée some of the chickpeas in the insert to thicken the mixture.

Add salt to taste, then stir in the lemon juice. Ladle into bowls, add a dollop of yogurt, and garnish with the chile slices and cilantro leaves.

SUGGESTED BEVERAGE: I would enjoy a light- to medium-bodied white wine, such as a Pinot Gris, Pinot Blanc, or Spanish Rueda or Albariño.

2 cups dried chickpeas

6 cups water

1 red onion, finely chopped

1/4 cup sesame or vegetable oil

1 tablespoon cumin seeds

1/4 teaspoon black peppercorns

4 whole cloves

4 green cardamom pods

1 1/2 teaspoons pure chile powder

1 1/2-inch piece fresh ginger, peeled and minced

1/2 teaspoon ground turmeric

1 teaspoon garam masala

1/2 teaspoon cayenne (optional)

Salt to taste

Juice of 1 lemon

Yogurt, for serving (optional)

3 fresh serrano chiles, seeded, deveined, and cut into julienne, for garnish

A few fresh cilantro leaves, for garnish

Creamy Dal

⤐ Serves 4 ⤏

In southern India, dal is traditionally served thin like a soup, then ladled over rice. But in northern India, where dal is traditionally scooped up with roti or served on rice, it is usually made thicker, almost the consistency of a porridge. I've suggested 4 to 5 cups of water so that you can make it thin like the southern Indians or thicker like a northern "stew." In addition, you can vary the heat intensity in the finished dish by the number of serrano chiles you add. Keep in mind that one serrano will add heat to the whole dish.

Thoroughly rinse the lentils, being sure to remove any small stones or dirt, then place them in the slow cooker insert and add the water (the amount will depend on the consistency you desire).

Cover and cook on low for 4 to 6 hours, until the lentils are tender. While the lentils are cooking, prepare the remaining ingredients.

In a sauté pan, melt the butter and add the chopped onion. Sauté until the onion is medium brown, about 10 minutes. Add the cumin seeds, mustard seeds, ginger, and chiles and continue cooking for another 5 minutes over medium heat. Add the tomato and continue to cook for another 5 minutes.

When the lentils are ready, add the sautéed onion mixture to the pot and stir together gently. Continue cooking just until all ingredients are heated through, 10 to 15 minutes.

Add a pinch of curry powder and salt to taste, then stir in the half-and-half.

Serve hot, garnished with sprigs of cilantro.

SUGGESTED BEVERAGE: Because of the richness of the cream in this dish, I could go with a light- to medium-bodied white wine, a good blanc de blanc (sparkling wine), or even a rosé.

1 cup dried lentils

4 to 5 cups water

1 tablespoon unsalted butter

1/2 yellow onion, chopped

1/4 teaspoon cumin seeds

1/4 teaspoon mustard seeds

1/2-inch piece fresh ginger, peeled and grated

1 or 2 serrano chiles, seeded, deveined, and cut into julienne

1 large tomato, chopped

Pinch of curry powder

Salt to taste

1/2 cup half-and-half or heavy cream

Several sprigs fresh cilantro, for garnish

Dal with Ground Cinnamon, Cloves, Cardamom, and Cumin

❧ Serves 4 ❧

Dal can be a soup or stew (depending on how much liquid you use) of dried lentils, vegetables, and seasonings. Traditionally served over rice in much of India, it is a staple of the Indian diet. Millions of variations exist from region to region and cook to cook. Here is just one of many variations. This recipe makes use of the Indian technique of adding some last-minute ingredients for freshness rather than subjecting them to the full cooking time.

Thoroughly rinse the lentils, being sure to remove any small stones or dirt, then place them in the slow cooker insert.

In an electric coffee mill or a mortar and pestle, grind the cinnamon, cloves, cardamom pods, cumin seeds, and turmeric to a fine powder.

Add the spices and water (the amount will depend upon the consistency you desire) to the slow cooker insert, cover, then cook on low for 4 to 6 hours or on high for 2 hours. Add salt to taste.

To make the tempering oil, heat the oil in a sauté pan and sauté the onion until beginning to brown, then add the garlic, ginger, and chile and cook just long enough to soften the chile, about 15 seconds.

Stir half of the tempering oil into the dal along with half of the cilantro and all of the lemon juice.

Ladle the dal into bowls and spoon what remains of the tempering oil over the top of each bowl. Sprinkle with the remaining cilantro and serve.

SUGGESTED BEVERAGE: Again, I would opt for one of those light- to medium-bodied, very chilled white wines, such as a light, French-style Chardonnay, a crisp Albariño, or perhaps a Pinot Blanc.

1 cup dried lentils

1-inch piece cinnamon

3 whole cloves

4 green cardamom pods

1 teaspoon cumin seeds

$1/2$ teaspoon ground turmeric

4 to 5 cups cold water

Salt to taste

Tempering Oil

2 tablespoons oil or ghee

1 onion, finely chopped

3 cloves garlic, finely chopped

1 tablespoon peeled, minced fresh ginger

1 fresh hot green chile, minced

$1/4$ cup fresh cilantro leaves

Juice of $1/2$ lemon or lime

STUFFED PEPPERS WITH YOGURT SAUCE

∼ Serves 4 ∼

Practically every country in the world has a recipe for stuffing peppers: Spain, Greece, Italy, Hungary, and Mexico, to name a few. India is no exception. The following recipe offers a variety of colors, textures, and flavors, with the stuffing being relatively mild and the raita-like sauce offering much of the dish's flavor and texture. For a really stunning presentation, garnish with a sprinkling of fresh pomegranate seeds, Mogul style.

Prepare the peppers by slicing off their tops and removing any seeds and veins from the inside.

To make the stuffing, grind the cumin and coriander seeds coarsely in an electric coffee mill or a mortar and pestle. In a sauté pan, melt the butter and sauté the onion and almonds just until lightly browned, 5 to 7 minutes. Add the ground spices and sauté for another minute. Thoroughly mix in the rice, spinach, and raisins and add salt to taste. The spinach should wilt and cook from the heat of the other ingredients.

Stuff the bell peppers with the rice mixture and place the peppers in the slow cooker insert. Pour in the water and cook on low for 4 hours, or until the peppers are tender when pierced with a fork. While the peppers are cooking, prepare the sauce.

To make the sauce, place the yogurt in a bowl. Grind the cumin and coriander seeds to a coarse powder in an electric coffee mill or a mortar and pestle. Mix them into the yogurt. Using a garlic press, press the garlic into the yogurt and mix in thoroughly.

Half an hour before serving, mix the cucumber, fresh mint, chiles and onion into the yogurt sauce and add salt to taste.

4 red, green, yellow, or purple bell peppers

Stuffing

1 teaspoon cumin seeds

1 teaspoon coriander seeds

1 tablespoon butter

1/2 cup chopped yellow onion

1/2 cup sliced almonds

2 cups cooked basmati rice

6 ounces fresh spinach leaves

1 cup raisins

Salt to taste

1 cup water

Sauce

2 cups plain yogurt

1 teaspoon cumin seeds

1 teaspoon coriander seeds

2 cloves garlic

1/2 cucumber, peeled and chopped

1 teaspoon chopped fresh mint

When the peppers are done, remove each one from the slow cooker insert and place in a pasta bowl (best for catching any juices), then slit it open and pour a generous stream of sauce over the top.

Sprinkle with the chopped cilantro and pomegranate seeds and serve.

SUGGESTED BEVERAGE: How about a glass of Prosecco?

1 or 2 fresh serrano chiles, seeded, deveined, and finely chopped

$1/2$ small red onion, finely chopped

Salt to taste

$1/4$ cup chopped fresh cilantro leaves, for garnish

$1/4$ cup pomegranate seeds (optional)

WAARI MUTH

~ Serves 4 to 6 ~

When most of us think of Indian food, we think of lentils or chickpeas as the legumes of choice. However, because most Indians are vegetarians, beans form an important protein source in the Indian diet. The array of beans that actually appears on the table in India is far vaster than we imagine. Waari muth is a Kashmiri recipe calling for black beans, similar to the kind of beans found in Mexican, Cuban, and Southwestern dishes. It's a simple dish, yet with the typical seasonings of the Indian subcontinent, and very nourishing. Serve either in a bowl by itself garnished with cilantro, or over rice.

Wash the beans thoroughly, then place them in the slow cooker insert with the water.

Using a mortar and pestle or an electric coffee mill, coarsely grind the fennel seeds, then add to the beans. Stir in the turmeric, ginger, and garam masala. Cover and cook on high for about 8 hours, or until the beans are tender.

Add the pepper flakes and salt to taste, then spoon individual portions into a bowl and top with a sprinkle of cilantro.

SUGGESTED BEVERAGE: I think I'd go for the "fire and ice" principle on this one: a crisp, chilled, medium-bodied aromatic white wine, such as a Gewürztraminer or an Albariño.

2 cups dried black beans

6 cups water

2 teaspoons fennel seeds

2 teaspoons turmeric powder

1 teaspoon ground ginger

1 teaspoon garam masala or curry powder

$1/2$ teaspoon red pepper flakes

Salt to taste

$1/4$ cup coarsely chopped fresh cilantro leaves, for garnish

POTATOES AND CARROTS IN COCONUT CURRY

⤙ Serves 4 to 6 ⤚

This is one of my all-time favorites in my repertoire of Indian dishes. The addition of coconut milk identifies it as a typical southern Indian dish, where coconut milk is a common ingredient. (Coconut milk is rarely found in the cooking of the colder, mountainous climate of northern India, where coconuts don't grow.) It can be made in about 5 hours and served hot, warm, or at room temperature, like a traditional potato salad. Cooking times will vary according to the type and size of potatoes you use.

Wash the potatoes thoroughly, then place them in the slow cooker insert and add the water. Cover and cook on low for 4 to 5 hours, or until the potatoes are fairly tender. (Cooking time will depend on the size and the type of potato you use. Tiny red potatoes, for instance, will probably cook in less than 4 hours, so use a fork to determine doneness. If your potatoes are fairly large, you may wish to cut them carefully into quarters before proceeding with the rest of the recipe.)

In a sauté pan, heat the oil and sauté the onion over medium-high heat until golden brown, about 10 minutes. Add the garlic, cumin seeds, and fennel seeds and continue cooking for another 2 to 3 minutes.

Add the onion, carrots, and curry powder to the potatoes, and carefully stir in the coconut cream. Recover and continue cooking for 1 hour.

Add salt to taste, then spoon the curry into a bowl or onto plates and garnish with the chile slices and cilantro.

Note: Coconut cream is a thicker version of coconut milk. It will say coconut "cream" right on the can. The mouthfeel of the cream is much richer than that of the milk, and as you might imagine, it is also higher in calories. You can substitute coconut milk for the cream in this recipe, but it is soooo good with the cream.

SUGGESTED BEVERAGE: I picture something chilled and white: Gewürztraminer or Pinot Gris, perhaps? Maybe even a citrusy New Zealand Sauvignon Blanc?

3 pounds red potatoes

1 cup water

2 tablespoons vegetable oil

1 onion, finely chopped

2 cloves garlic, coarsely chopped

2 tablespoons cumin seeds

2 teaspoons fennel seeds

1 pound carrots, sliced into rounds

2 tablespoons curry powder

1 can (about 14 ounces) coconut cream (see Note below)

Salt to taste

4 serrano chiles, seeded, deveined, and cut into julienne, for garnish

1/4 cup chopped fresh cilantro leaves, for garnish

MOGUL EGGPLANT

≈ Serves 4 ≈

Muslims from Persia and Central Asia invaded India from the north and ruled much of the country during the sixteenth to eighteenth centuries. As a culture, they are called "Mogul." They brought with them a period of relative peace and affluence, unifying the native cultures and cuisines of India with those of the Persian Empire. Adding yogurt to a dish is a Mogul touch, as is sealing food with dough in a clay pot and cooking it directly over the coals of a fire. The following recipe is a typical Mogul-style dish, cooked in your slow cooker instead of over a fire. Add the yogurt at the last minute to avoid curdling. (Note: If you cut the eggplant into cubes, the dish makes an excellent sauce for pasta.) Serve with basmati rice.

In an electric coffee mill or a mortar and pestle, grind the cumin seeds and cloves to a fine powder. Add the ginger and garlic and continue to grind until a powdery paste forms.

Place the eggplant slices in the slow cooker insert.

In a bowl, combine the ground spice—ginger mixture, garam masala, turmeric, paprika, cayenne, and crushed tomatoes, mix thoroughly, and then pour the spiced sauce over the eggplant slices, spreading it evenly over them.

Cover and cook on low for about 4 hours, or until the eggplant is tender and cuts easily. When the eggplant is done, turn off the heat, remove the lid, and allow the dish to sit for 10 minutes. Carefully mix in the yogurt and add salt to taste

Serve hot, sprinkling the fresh cilantro and chiles over the top of the eggplant.

SUGGESTED BEVERAGE: Once again I revert to my chilled, light- to medium-bodied white wine on this one. A rosé, I think, would also work nicely. Even a fruity, young red wine might go well.

1 teaspoon cumin seeds

6 whole cloves

1 tablespoon peeled, minced fresh ginger

2 teaspoons minced garlic

2 small eggplants, peeled and sliced into quarters vertically

2 teaspoons garam masala

1 teaspoon ground turmeric

1 tablespoon paprika

1/4 teaspoon cayenne (optional)

1 (28-ounce) can crushed tomatoes

2 cups plain yogurt

Salt to taste

1/4 cup chopped fresh cilantro leaves, for garnish

2 fresh serrano chiles, seeded, deveined, and cut into julienne, for garnish

Minted Potato and Chickpea Curry

~ Serves 4 ~

This potato and chickpea curry, with its coconut milk and sugar, is more characteristic of southern Indian cooking than northern. The chickpeas themselves take a nice, long cook, while the remaining ingredients are added about an hour before serving.

Thoroughly rinse the chickpeas and place them in the slow cooker insert along with the water. Cover and cook on low for 6 to 8 hours, or until the chickpeas are just tender.

Remove the cover and gently stir in the chile powder, turmeric, potato, tomatoes, coconut milk, and sugar. Add salt to taste, replace the cover, and continue cooking for about 1 hour longer, or until the potatoes are tender.

Spoon into bowls and top each serving with 1 tablespoon each of chopped mint and cilantro, and a pinch of chopped jalapeño.

SUGGESTED BEVERAGE: Surprise! Why not try a sparkling Shiraz with this dish?

2 cups dried chickpeas

6 cups water

2 teaspoons pure chile powder

1 teaspoon turmeric

1 russet potato, peeled and diced

2 tomatoes, coarsely chopped

$1/2$ cup unsweetened coconut milk or coconut cream

1 to 2 teaspoons palm sugar or brown sugar

Salt to taste

$1/4$ cup chopped fresh mint leaves

$1/4$ cup chopped fresh cilantro leaves

1 jalapeño chile, seeds and veins removed, finely chopped

SPICY INDIAN LENTIL AND TOMATO SOUP

❧ Serves 4 ❧

One of the beautiful things about traditional Indian cooking is that each cook grinds her own spices, and each dish therefore bears the unique thumbprint of its creator. Freshly ground spices give this simple soup a gourmet touch.

Wash the lentils thoroughly, being sure to remove any small stones or dirt. Place them, along with the water, in the slow cooker insert.

In an electric coffee mill or a mortar and pestle, grind the cumin seeds, coriander seeds, and peppercorns to a coarse powder.

In a bowl, combine the ground spices, turmeric, tamarind concentrate, tomatoes, and garlic; add to the lentils.

Cook, covered, on low for 5 to 6 hours, or until the lentils are quite tender and the flavors have melded.

Add the corn and salt to taste just before serving so that the corn retains its fresh flavor and texture.

To make the tempering oil, heat the ghee in a frying pan, then add the mustard seeds and broken chile and sauté until the seeds begin to pop. Quickly remove from the heat and drizzle a tiny bit over each bowl of soup.

Sprinkle with the fresh cilantro and serve.

SUGGESTED BEVERAGE: Any chilled, aromatic white wine will do nicely here.

1 cup dried lentils

6 cups water

1 teaspoon cumin seeds

1 tablespoon coriander seeds

8 black peppercorns

1 teaspoon ground turmeric

1 teaspoon tamarind concentrate
(see Note on pages 51–52)

3 large tomatoes, coarsely
chopped

3 cloves garlic, finely minced

Kernels cut from 2 ears fresh
corn, or 1 cup frozen corn

Salt to taste

Tempering Oil

2 teaspoons ghee

2 teaspoons black mustard seeds

1 dried red chile, broken into bits

1/4 cup chopped fresh cilantro
leaves

TOMATO, RICE, AND CORIANDER SOUP

⤞ Serves 4 ⤝

Another delicious Indian soup, similar to the Spicy Indian Lentil and Tomato Soup (page 26), but with rice and a very different blend of spices.

Using the side of a chef's knife, smash together the ginger and garlic, being careful not to cut your fingers.

In an electric coffee mill or a mortar and pestle, grind the cinnamon, cloves, cardamom, peppercorns, and cumin seeds to a coarse powder.

In a skillet, heat the ghee and sauté the onion over medium-high heat until brown, about 10 minutes, and then add the garlic, ginger, and spices to the onion. Continue to cook for 2 to 3 minutes more.

Place the onion mixture, carrots, tomatoes, water, and rice in the slow cooker insert. Cover and cook on low for 4 to 6 hours, or until the rice and carrots are thoroughly tender. Stir in the lemon juice and add salt to taste.

Ladle into bowls and garnish with the chopped cilantro and chiles. Add a dollop of yogurt and serve immediately.

SUGGESTED BEVERAGE: A bright, light fruity Pinot Gris would do nicely with this soup.

1-inch piece fresh ginger, peeled and finely minced

3 cloves garlic, finely minced

1 cinnamon stick

4 cloves

6 green cardamom pods

8 black peppercorns

2 teaspoons cumin seeds

1 tablespoon ghee or vegetable oil

1 onion, finely chopped

2/3 cup peeled, sliced carrots

3 tomatoes, coarsely chopped

6 cups water

2 tablespoons brown basmati rice

3 tablespoons fresh lemon juice

Salt to taste

1/4 cup chopped fresh cilantro leaves, for garnish

2 serrano chiles, seeded, deveined, and thinly sliced, for garnish

Yogurt, for serving (optional)

Mexico and the Southwest

What most of us think of as "Mexican" food today includes some fairly simple ingredients: chicken, beef, lots of cheese, tomato sauces, and peppers, cooked in a limited number of ways.

But real Mexican cooking is a skillful blending of ingredients from the Old and New Worlds. The flavors are those used by the indigenous peoples of the Americas—unsweetened chocolate, peppers, potatoes, beans, tomatoes, and native herbs and seasonings—with a rich overlay of ingredients brought originally by Spanish explorers and missionaries: beef, chicken, lamb, goat, dairy products, wine, and wheat, to name a few.

The combination of these ingredients in the hands of Mexican cooks has produced some of the most exciting and complex dishes on the face of the planet.

According to legend, for instance, *mole poblano*, Mexico's national festive dish, was created in the sixteenth century by nuns at the Convent of Santa Rosa in Puebla de los Angeles. The story goes that the archbishop was planning a visit and the nuns had nothing suitably grand to serve him, so guided by divine inspiration, they began chopping and mixing pantry ingredients they had on hand: chiles, chocolate, nuts, day-old bread, and a host of other ingredients.

Whether the legend is true or not, its theme of loving hands combining the ingredients of two very different cultures and peoples into one magnificent creation is accurate.

Many dishes in Mexico—both ancient and modern—were baked in an oven in earthenware *cazuelas* for long periods of time, making dishes of both Mexico and the Southwestern United States (so influenced by Mexico) perfect candidates for adaptation to slow cookers.

WINES WITH MEXICAN FOOD

Matching wines with often complex Mexican flavors can be just about as intimidating as matching wines to complex, often fiery Indian cuisine. Not surprisingly, many of the types of wines that work well with Indian food also work well with Mexican foods.

Dry or off-dry aromatic whites such as Gewürztraminer, Riesling, Pinot Blanc and Gris, Müller-Thurgau, Albariño, and Chenin Blanc can cool the heat of dishes with lots of chiles and spices. As with Indian food, Prosecco, cava, champagne, and other sparkling wines can make refreshing pairings.

In general, I would avoid pairing tannic wines with foods rich in chiles and spices, but you never know. The sweetness of a *mole poblano*, for instance, might render it a good pairing with the right Cab, Nebbiolo, or Garnacha.

Wines from Spain and California might be especially good choices for your Mexican and Southwestern dishes, but you can also draw upon some of the increasingly wonderful wines being made in the Southwestern United States. One of my favorite sparkling wines, for instance, is made by the Gruet family (of Champagne fame) in southwestern New Mexico. It is very good and very reasonably priced. There are also growing fine wine industries in both Arizona (centered around Sonoita) and New Mexico.

Although winemaking in Mexico was suppressed for all but the clergy for two or three hundred years, a modern-day boutique wine industry has blossomed in the Valle de Guadalupe, just an hour and a half south of San Diego in Baja California. If you have an opportunity to taste some of the wines of this region, by all means, take it. A growing number are very good. You can occasionally find Mexican wines in American specialty wine shops, too, especially if you live in the Southwest—or you might just want to take a road trip through Mexican wine country.

MY FAVORITE CHILI

≈ Serves 6 to 8 ≈

Chili, a quintessential slow cooker meal, is not a traditional Mexican dish. Rather, it seems to be Southwestern in its inception. It is sort of a combination of the dried beans and chiles so readily available in the Southwest with the wonderful spices brought by Europeans to Mexico. This particular version is generously seasoned with spices and chili powder and has been pieced together by me over the course of a few years. The following recipe makes a big mess o' chili and is best done in a 6- or 7-quart slow cooker.

Thoroughly wash the beans and place them, along with the water, in the slow cooker insert. Grind the allspice, cinnamon, oregano, cumin, aniseed, and coriander seeds in an electric coffee mill or a mortar and pestle and add to the beans. Cover and cook on low for 6 hours, or until the beans are tender.

Add the diced onion, garlic, tomatoes, cocoa powder, and chili powder to the beans and continue cooking for 2 hours.

About half an hour before serving, add the red and green bell pepper and corn kernels to the beans so they retain their crisp, fresh taste and texture.

Ladle into bowls and top each bowl with a dollop of sour cream and a sprinkling of green onion and cilantro.

SUGGESTED BEVERAGE: Although you could also choose fruity red wine to drink with this dish, I would prefer a good Mexican beer.

2 cups dried kidney, pinto, pinquito, or pink beans

6 cups water

6 allspice berries

1 stick cinnamon

$1/2$ teaspoon dried Mexican oregano

$1/2$ teaspoon cumin seeds

$1/4$ teaspoon aniseed

$1/2$ teaspoon coriander seeds

$1/2$ onion, diced

3 cloves garlic, finely minced

1 (28-ounce) can crushed tomatoes

$1/4$ cup unsweetened cocoa powder

1 to 2 tablespoons chili powder

$1/4$ cup diced red bell pepper

$1/4$ cup diced green bell pepper

$1/2$ cup fresh or frozen corn kernels

$1/2$ cup sour cream or nonfat yogurt

$1/4$ cup thinly sliced green onions, green part only, for garnish

$1/2$ cup chopped fresh cilantro leaves, for garnish

Vegetable Amarillo

Amarillo means "yellow" in Spanish, and it is also the name of one of the seven classic moles, or sauces, from Oaxaca, known as "The Land of Seven Moles." Though far from yellow (it's more of a brick red), it can be used as a base for a delicious and very spicy vegetable stew that can stand alone or be served over rice to cut its heat.

To make the sauce, wash the dried chiles well (they are often dusty). Toast them in a frying pan briefly and lightly on each side. Do not allow them to burn or they will become bitter. When they cool, remove their stems, slit them open, and remove the seeds and veins. Tear them into pieces and place them in the slow cooker insert. Cover with the water.

In an electric coffee mill or a mortar and pestle, grind the allspice, cloves, and cumin seeds to a powder, then add to the chiles.

Add the garlic, oregano, oil, raisins, onion, tortilla, and tomatillos. Cover and cook on high for about 1 hour.

Using an immersion blender, blend the mixture as smooth as possible right in the slow cooker insert. Be sure to keep the head of the blender below the surface of the sauce or you will splatter sauce all over the place. (Wear an apron just in case!) The sauce can be made 1 day ahead of time.

Sauce

12 dried guajillo chiles

3 cups water

4 whole allspice berries

4 whole cloves

1/4 teaspoon cumin seeds

9 cloves garlic, peeled

1 tablespoon dried Mexican oregano

2 tablespoons oil (sesame has good flavor)

1/4 cup raisins

1/2 onion, cut in half and lightly charred under the broiler

1 corn tortilla, torn into pieces

3 tomatillos, washed, husked, and quartered

To make the vegetables, add the chayote, potatoes, and butternut squash to the sauce in the slow cooker insert. Recover and cook on low for 3 to 4 hours, or until the potatoes are tender but still hold their shape.

Add the sliced mushrooms, orange juice and zest, and green beans and continue cooking for 30 to 40 minutes, just until the beans are al dente.

Serve topped with crumbled feta and chopped cilantro.

SUGGESTED BEVERAGE: Try a young, fruity red wine with some body, such as a Zinfandel or a Grenache, or even a rosé.

Vegetables

1 large chayote, peeled and cut into 1-inch chunks

1 pound red potatoes, unpeeled and cut into 1-inch chunks

$1/2$ pound butternut squash, peeled and cut into 1-inch chunks

3 portobello mushrooms, thickly sliced

Juice and zest of 1 orange

6 ounces green beans, trimmed and halved

Garnishes

$1/2$ pound Mexican queso fresco or feta cheese, crumbled

$1/4$ cup chopped fresh cilantro leaves

Slow-Cooked Grits with Chile and Cheese

~ Serves 2 to 4 ~

Grits, a traditional Southern breakfast dish, are often served topped with butter and cheese. They fill hungry bellies and stick to the ribs for many hours. Technically, grits are coarsely ground hominy, and they are white in color, while polenta is ground, dried yellow corn. But in the United States (outside the Deep South), the two are often used interchangeably. It's best if you can find the stone-ground real thing, but if not, you can use the instant grits that are available in nearly every grocery store or mail-order them from a source that specializes in grains, such as Bob's Red Mill in Oregon. I recommend using a 2- to 3-quart slow cooker so that your grits don't dry out overnight.

Place the grits, salt, and water in the slow cooker insert. Cover and cook on low overnight, about 8 hours.

In the morning, simply stir in the chiles, adjust the salt to taste, and stir in half the cheese. Spoon up a bowlful for each person, then top with the remaining cheese.

SUGGESTED BEVERAGE: No wine here, but a good, hearty cup of coffee at breakfast time or a Mexican beer at lunch or dinner.

1 cup grits

$1/2$ teaspoon salt

4 cups water

1 (7-ounce) can diced green chiles

1 cup grated sharp cheddar or smoked gouda (or a combination)

SPAGHETTI SQUASH WITH MEXICAN SPICES

≈ Serves 4 ≈

The spaghetti squash gets its name from the fact that its insides, when cooked, separate into spaghetti-like strands that can be used in exactly the same way you would use spaghetti. You can either top the strands with Tomato-Mushroom Sauce (page 63) or toss it with your favorite Mexican spices. Choose a squash that will fit in the slow cooker insert. If need be, the squash can be halved to fit, but the cooking time will be shorter.

Wash the spaghetti squash, then place it in the slow cooker insert and add the water. Cover and cook on low for 5 to 6 hours, or until the squash is tender when pierced with a fork. Remove the squash from the slow cooker and allow it to cool slightly while you prepare the spices and butter.

Using an electric coffee mill or a mortar and pestle, crush the cumin seeds, coriander seeds, cloves, cinnamon, and red pepper flakes together. Leave some texture to them rather than powdering them.

Melt the butter in the microwave or on the stove top. Using a garlic press, press the garlic into the butter. Stir in the spices and remove from the heat.

Carefully halve the squash lengthwise (it will give off steam) and remove and discard the seeds. Working over a bowl, scrape out the flesh with a fork, loosening and separating the strands as you remove them from the skin. Toss with the butter and spices and add salt to taste.

To serve, garnish each portion with cilantro and sprinkle with cheese.

SUGGESTED BEVERAGE: I'd like something nice and light with this dish, with a hint of spice to complement the seasonings. A chilled Gewürztraminer or even a Mexican Chenin Blanc would be perfect.

1 spaghetti squash

1 cup water

1 teaspoon cumin seeds

1 teaspoon coriander seeds

4 whole cloves

1 teaspoon ground cinnamon

$1/8$ teaspoon red pepper flakes

4 tablespoons unsalted butter or olive oil

3 cloves garlic, minced

Salt to taste

$1/4$ cup chopped fresh cilantro leaves, for garnish

$1/2$ cup Mexican queso fresco or feta cheese

MEXICAN BLACK BEAN SOUP

⤶ Serves 4 to 6 ⤷

I think of black beans in Mexican cuisine as an almost upscale replacement for pinto beans, but in actual fact, they have been part of the meso–American culinary repertoire for thousands of years. This is a simple, flavorful, nutritious one-pot meal.

Thoroughly wash the beans and place them, along with the water and onion, in the slow cooker insert. Cover and cook on low for about 8 hours, or until the beans are tender.

Using a handheld immersion blender, purée some of the beans to thicken the soup. (How much you purée depends on how much texture you'd like remaining in the soup.)

Add salt to taste, then ladle into bowls. Top each serving with some crumbled cheese, a sprinkle of cilantro, and some tortilla strips.

SUGGESTED BEVERAGE: This is a relatively mild dish, so I'd choose a chilled, medium-bodied white wine, perhaps with a little spice. A Gewürztraminer or even an off-dry Muscat Canelli would work well. A beer would do nicely, too.

2 cups dried black beans

8 cups water

1 white onion, finely diced

Salt to taste (smoked, if possible)

$1/2$ cup crumbled Mexican queso fresco or feta cheese

$1/4$ cup chopped fresh cilantro leaves, for garnish

4 corn tortillas, sliced into $1/8$-inch-wide strips and fried until crisp, or $1/3$ cup corn chips, crumbled into large pieces, for garnish

RUSTIC POTATO AND POBLANO GRATIN

❧ Serves 4 ❧

Potatoes and chiles are "New World" stuff, and yet, as it turns out, they have nourished millions of people around the world since they were brought to the "Old World" by European explorers just a few hundred years ago. Here is a simple dish combining the Old World and New World ingredients, stewed together in the pot—in this case, the slow cooker. Unlike conventional scalloped potatoes baked in a gratin pan, where "design" matters, I recommend gently stirring these potatoes once or twice during their cooking time to evenly distribute the good stuff and ensure even cooking.

To roast the chiles, place them on a baking sheet lined with aluminum foil about 8 inches from the broiler. Broil them until the skin blisters and turns black on both sides. (Do not burn the chiles themselves.) Remove the baking sheet from the oven and quickly cover the chiles with a clean dish towel. Let them sit, covered, until they are cool. Using a paring knife or your fingers, carefully peel off the skins, then slit one side and remove the seeds and veins. Cut the chiles into thin strips.

Melt the butter in the bottom of the slow cooker insert.

Place a layer of the sliced potatoes in the bottom of the slow cooker insert. (I use a bit more than one potato per layer.) Sprinkle lightly with freshly ground smoked or regular salt. Place a thin layer of cheese (about one-third of the cheese) on top of the potatoes. Place about half of the chile strips on top of the cheese. Repeat with another layer of potatoes, salt, cheese, and chiles. Finish with a layer of potatoes.

Pour the water over the potatoes. Cover and cook on low for about $1^{1}/_{2}$ hours, or until the potatoes are beginning to get tender.

Using a garlic press, press the garlic into the cream; pour the cream mixture over the potatoes, then add a last layer of cheese sprinkled with a bit of salt. Recover and cook for another 3 hours, or until the sauce has thickened and the potatoes are quite tender.

SUGGESTED BEVERAGE: A dry white wine of light to medium body would work for me with this dish. A French or Mexican Chardonnay or even a cava (Spanish sparkling wine) would also be nice.

Ingredients

- 4 poblano chiles
- 1 tablespoon unsalted butter or olive oil
- 4 large russet potatoes, peeled and thinly sliced
- Salt to taste (smoked, if possible)
- $^{1}/_{4}$ pound flavorful jack or sharp cheddar cheese, grated or sliced
- $^{1}/_{2}$ cup water
- 3 cloves garlic, peeled
- 1 cup heavy cream or half-and-half

STACKED CAULIFLOWER ENCHILADA
WITH GREEN CHILE SAUCE

❧ Serves 4 to 6 ❧

Most of us are familiar with "rolled" enchiladas: some kind of savory filling rolled up in a tortilla, then baked. But a stacked enchilada is even easier to make, and the results, especially when done in a slow cooker, are a lot like a casserole. A layer of corn or flour tortillas, a layer of fresh vegetables, another layer of tortillas, another layer of filling, and so on until the slow cooker insert is a bit over half full. Then a nice long, slow cook that allows all the juicy vegetable flavors to meld and blend. You can certainly vary the type of vegetables according to the season and what's in your garden or farmers' market at any given time. This is great freshly cooked and is even better as leftovers.

Trim and core the cauliflower, then wash and slice the head vertically. (You will be placing it in layers in the casserole, so you want the pieces fairly thin.) Pull the onion layers apart.

In a large bowl, combine the cauliflower, onion, olives, tomatoes, and beans using your hands.

Oil the inside of the slow cooker insert. Place 2 or 3 overlapping tortillas in the bottom of the insert. Add a layer of half the mixed vegetables and top it with a generous sprinkling of cheese (about one-third of the cheese). Pour ¹/₂ cup of the enchilada sauce over the layer.

Add another layer of tortillas, then half of the remaining vegetables and another one-third of the cheese. Pour on another ¹/₂ cup of sauce. Finish with an additional layer of tortillas and the remaining 2¹/₂ cups sauce. (Even though you may appear to have an excess of sauce, much of it is absorbed into the tortillas and vegetables as they cook.)

1 head cauliflower

1 white onion, cut vertically into 8 pieces

1 cup sliced pitted California olives, drained

2 tomatoes, coarsely chopped

1 (15-ounce) can black beans, drained

6 to 9 corn tortillas

¹/₂ pound smoked or regular cheddar or Monterey Jack cheese, grated

1 (28-ounce) can green enchilada sauce

¹/₄ cup chopped fresh cilantro leaves, for garnish

¹/₂ cup sour cream, for garnish

Cover and cook on low for 5 to 6 hours, or until the cauliflower is tender. Top the casserole with the remaining cheese, cover, and cook for an additional 30 minutes, or until the cheese is melted.

Turn off the heat and allow the contents of the insert to sit for 10 to 15 minutes to set, then carefully scoop up generous individual servings of the enchilada into bowls. Top each serving with a sprinkle of cilantro and a dollop of sour cream.

SUGGESTED BEVERAGE: A nice, light, summery rosé would be great with this dish.

Sopa de Ajo

❧ Serves 4 ❧

There is a Mexican restaurant in my town that specializes in caldos, *or Mexican broth-based soups like this* sopa de ajo. *Everyone goes there to get take-out* caldo *when they feel a cold or flu coming on, but most of the time, everyone goes there just because they like* caldo!

Place the water and garlic in the slow cooker insert, cover, and cook on low for 6 to 8 hours, or until the garlic is quite tender.

Add the bread to the broth and allow to soften for about 10 minutes, then purée the garlic and bread using a handheld immersion blender. Add the olive oil and salt to taste.

To serve, place some of the avocado, oregano, cheese, tomato, and green onions in the bottom of each bowl, then ladle in the broth over the ingredients. Top each bowl with a sprinkle of cilantro.

SUGGESTED BEVERAGE: I would enjoy a light-bodied white wine or possibly a light, fruity, young red wine with this soup.

6 cups water

2 large heads garlic, cloves separated and peeled

4 slices French or country bread

1/4 cup fruity olive oil

Salt to taste

1 ripe avocado, cut into 1/2-inch dice

1 teaspoon dried Mexican oregano

3 ounces Mexican queso fresco or feta cheese, crumbled

1 ripe tomato, diced

4 green onions, thinly sliced, green part only

1/4 cup chopped fresh cilantro leaves, for garnish

MEXICAN CHOCOLATE PUDDING CAKE

∾ Serves 6 ∾

Making puddings is one of the tasks the slow cooker does especially well. This scrumptious blend of flavors often found in Mexican chocolate and desserts is a wonderful ending to a meal, or an afternoon or evening snack all by itself. I like to eat it hot, warm, or at room temperature, topped with a generous dollop of whipped cream and dusted with cocoa powder or grated chocolate.

To make the pudding, in a food processor, finely grind the chocolate. Add the butter, brown sugar, flour, buttermilk, eggs, vanilla and maple extracts, apple pie spice, coffee, baking powder, and a pinch of salt and process until the mixture is relatively smooth. (There will still be tiny flecks of chocolate in the mixture.)

Pour the mixture into the slow cooker insert, cover, and cook on low for about 2 hours, or until the edges are set. The center of the pudding will still appear to be somewhat uncooked, and this is fine.

Once the pudding is done, with a hand mixer or an immersion blender, whip the cream until frothy, then add a tablespoon or two of confectioner's sugar (to taste). Continue whipping until peaks form.

To serve, spoon a serving of the pudding cake into a bowl, then top with a dollop of softly whipped cream and garnish with grated chocolate.

SUGGESTED BEVERAGE: Cold milk, hot coffee, or a glass of tawny port would be perfect with this pudding cake.

Pudding

8 ounces bittersweet chocolate, cut into chunks

1/2 cup (1 stick) unsalted butter, cut into pieces

1/2 cup packed dark brown sugar

1/4 cup all-purpose flour

1 1/2 cups buttermilk

4 large eggs

1 teaspoon pure vanilla extract

1/2 teaspoon pure maple extract

1 tablespoon apple pie spice

1 tablespoon finely ground coffee

1/2 teaspoon baking powder

Pinch of salt

1 cup heavy cream

1 to 2 tablespoons confectioner's sugar

Grated chocolate or unsweetened cocoa powder, for garnish

Asia

One of the problems with creating Asian-inspired dishes for the slow cooker is that traditionally in Asian cultures, most dishes are cooked quickly on the stove top or over a fire.

Everyone, for instance, is familiar with the Chinese wok and its relatives that appear throughout Asia. Asian culinary traditions in general contain far fewer long, slow-cooked one-pot meals than do those of the Western world.

The Korean-Style Black Beans, Soy-Braised Potatoes, and Potatoes and Peas in Red Curry Sauce could all be considered exceptions to this quick-cooking, stove top tradition. And the Japanese-Style Braised Tofu is so darn good that I just couldn't leave it out, even if it takes only a couple of hours to cook. It offers the perfect opportunity to put

something easy on to cook when you come home from work, so you can put your feet up, savor a glass of wine, and have dinner on the table without much ado an hour or two later. The Butternut Squash in Green Curry Sauce is visually exciting, and the Green Vegetable Curry, though clearly of stove top origins, works well.

In this chapter, I have drawn from a number of very different culinary traditions, from the soy-based sauces often found in Japanese and Korean dishes to the unique seasonings found in Malaysian food and the more Indian-like flavors of Thai cooking.

Thai curries are in some ways similar to those of their Indian neighbors, but with the addition of certain characteristic Thai ingredients, such as lemon grass, galangal (a type of ginger), and coconut milk—ingredients that are not easily found in the United States (unless, of course, you live near a good Asian market). So do what Asian cooks often do: use curry pastes that have been prepared by someone else, someone who specializes in making spice pastes. In Thailand, you can often buy prepared pastes at the local shop or in the market. Here, you can often find different Thai curry pastes on the shelves of Whole Foods or other cosmopolitan supermarket chains.

WINES WITH ASIAN FOOD

Although it may be difficult to try to lump the foods of a region as vast as Asia into one big category for pairing with wines, you can probably make a few assumptions that apply to the interesting flavors many of them share in common.

Many of the flavors we like best in Asian foods, including soy sauce, chiles, ginger, lemon grass, and galangal, can make a serious dent in the flavor profile of a good wine. In general, some of the same principles that apply to pairing wines with Mexican and Indian cuisines apply to pairing them with Asian flavors. Wines to avoid would be heavy, oaky Chardonnays and wines such as Cabernets and Merlots with lots of tannins. And wines that might work well with Asian flavors would be your crisp, clean, acidic wines, such as New Zealand Sauvignon Blancs, Pinot Grigios from Italy, crisp whites from British Columbia, and some northern Italian whites. The same goes for aromatic white wines: Gewürztraminer, Riesling, and Viognier. Fruity red wines (as opposed to the more tannic varietals) like Syrah and Zinfandel might make good matches. And, just as with Indian and Mexican foods, anything with bubbles in it ought to go well.

SOY-BRAISED POTATOES

❧ Serves 4 ❧

Wherever they are grown around the world, potatoes fill the belly and warm the heart. Although potato dishes are less common in Asian countries than in Western and Eastern European countries, they can still fill the belly and warm the heart, Asian style. A crisp green salad would make a fine accompaniment to the dish.

Place the potatoes and water in the slow cooker insert. (The smaller the pieces, the faster they will cook. Also, the greater the surface area of the potato that is exposed, the more the sauce will be soaked up, and the more flavorful your potatoes will be.)

Cover and cook on low for about 3 hours, or until the potatoes are somewhat tender when pierced with a fork, stirring now and again to keep all sides of the potatoes cooking evenly.

In a small bowl, combine the sugar, soy sauce, sesame oil, and garlic and pour over the potatoes, tossing thoroughly to coat all sides. Recover and continue cooking for about 30 minutes longer.

Serve garnished with the toasted sesame seeds, sliced green onion, and red pepper flakes.

SUGGESTED BEVERAGE: I'm thinking perhaps a lighter-style Roussanne or Rhône-style white blend from California.

2 pounds red or white rose potatoes, washed and halved or quartered

$1/2$ cup water

1 tablespoon sugar

$1/4$ cup soy sauce

1 tablespoon toasted sesame oil

2 cloves garlic, peeled and crushed

1 tablespoon sesame seeds, toasted, for garnish

1 green onion, thinly sliced, green part only, for garnish

Red pepper flakes, for garnish (optional)

POTATOES AND PEAS IN RED CURRY SAUCE

❧ Serves 4 ❧

Thai curries differ from northern Indian curries in that they add some typically Thai ingredients, such as dried red chiles, onion, garlic, coconut milk, galangal, lemon grass, and kaffir lime, to the warm Indian spice blends. They are categorized as red, yellow, or green based on the kind of chile or ingredients used in them (but not necessarily by the color of the finished product), and they have an element of sweetness to them that is lacking in some Indian curries. They can be made from scratch, but most Thai home cooks today rely on either commercially prepared pastes or pastes prepared by a vendor down the street. Many supermarkets in the United States carry Thai curry pastes. And if you really want to save time, you can purchase a jar or two of Thai Red Curry Simmer Sauce (Whole Foods and Trader Joe's are two good bets) and save yourself the trouble of doing any mixing at all! Most Thai curries, including this one, should be served with steamed rice.

Wash the potatoes thoroughly and place them, along with the onion, in the slow cooker insert.

Mix the coconut cream, red curry paste, sugar, and soy sauce together and pour over the potatoes. Cover and cook on low for about 3 hours, or until the potatoes are somewhat tender when pierced with a fork.

Add the sweet potato, cover, and continue to cook on low for another 2 to 3 hours, or until all the vegetables are tender. Add the peas along with salt to taste and continue to cook, uncovered, for 15 minutes longer.

To serve, sprinkle each portion with 1 to 2 tablespoons cashews and some cilantro.

SUGGESTED BEVERAGE: A Sauvignon Blanc with a hint of citrus ought to complement this dish quite nicely.

2 pounds small red or yellow potatoes, cut into 1^1/$_2$-inch pieces if necessary

1 yellow onion, sliced vertically into sections

1 can (about 14 ounces) coconut cream (see Note on page 22)

2 to 3 tablespoons red curry paste

2 tablespoons palm sugar or brown sugar

1 teaspoon soy sauce

1 large sweet potato, peeled and cut into 1^1/$_2$-inch pieces

1 cup fresh or frozen green peas

Salt to taste

^{1}/$_2$ cup dry-roasted cashews, for garnish

^{1}/$_4$ cup chopped fresh cilantro leaves, for garnish

MARGARET HUGHES'S GREEN VEGETABLE CURRY

≈ Serves 4 ≈

My dear friend Martha Deaton was raised in Malaysia, where she and her sisters learned to cook traditional Malaysian dishes from their mother. Martha's sister, Margaret Hughes, has built a thriving London catering business based on the dishes of her homeland. The following is one of her most popular recipes. Although this dish, like so many Asian dishes, is traditionally prepared on top of the stove, I think it works well in the slow cooker. See what you think. Serve it hot, on a bed of steamed rice.

Place the eggplant in the slow cooker insert with $1/2$ cup water. Cover and cook on low for about 3 hours, or until the chunks are somewhat tender.

In an electric coffee mill or a mortar and pestle, grind the coriander, fennel, and cumin seeds to a powder.

In a blender, combine the onion, lemon grass, galangal, ground spices, 1 teaspoon salt, coconut cream, tamarind concentrate, the remaining cup of water, soy sauce, bell pepper, nuts, chiles, and oil until you have a nice, fragrant sauce. Set aside.

When the eggplant pieces are nearly tender, add the green beans and cabbage and continue to cook for another 30 minutes, or until the green beans and cabbage are also tender.

About 10 minutes before serving, stir in the sauce and add salt to taste. Serve hot.

Note: Ingredients such as ground galangal (or fresh galangal root, if you're lucky enough to find it), tamarind concentrate, and lemon grass can be found at Asian markets and sometimes at regular supermarkets

1 eggplant, peeled and cut into 1-inch cubes

$1^1/2$ cups water

1 tablespoon coriander seeds

1 tablespoon fennel seeds

1 teaspoon cumin seeds

1 onion, peeled and cut into chunks

2-inch piece lemon grass, sliced (use the tender bottom 2 inches of the stem), or 1 teaspoon ground dried lemon grass

1 teaspoon ground galangal (sometimes called Thai ginger; see Note below)

1 teaspoon salt, plus more to taste

1 (about 14 ounces) can coconut cream (see Note on page 22)

1 to 2 tablespoons tamarind concentrate (see Note below)

1 tablespoon soy sauce

(continued)

where there is a significant Asian population. For an especially quick and easy version of this dish, purchase generic green curry paste at an Asian market instead of making the sauce from scratch.

SUGGESTED BEVERAGE: Something white, crisp, and refreshing, perhaps a Canadian Gewürztraminer or a New Zealand Sauvignon Blanc.

1 tablespoon soy sauce

1 green bell pepper, seeded, deveined, and cut into chunks

¼ cup macadamia nuts

3 serrano or jalapeño chiles, stemmed, seeded, deveined, and cut into chunks

1 tablespoon vegetable oil

12 ounces fresh green beans, trimmed and cut into 1½-inch pieces

3 ounces napa cabbage, thinly sliced (about 3 cups)

KOREAN-STYLE BLACK BEANS

❧ Serves 6 ❧

You might consider this simple recipe the Korean version of New England baked beans: sweet and salty at the same time. The beans are slow-cooked to give the flavors time to meld, and served accompanied by some cooked greens, a salad, or some rice for a complete protein.

Wash the beans thoroughly, then place them in the slow cooker insert along with the water.

Mix together the soy sauce, sugar, and sesame oil and pour over the beans, stirring in thoroughly.

Cover and cook on low for 6 to 8 hours, or until the beans are tender.

SUGGESTED BEVERAGE: Perhaps something with bubbles, such as Prosecco or a sparkling Californian wine. And if all else fails, a good ol' beer would complement this dish nicely (and would be more traditional than wine as an accompaniment).

2 cups dried black beans

6 cups water

½ cup soy sauce

1 tablespoon sugar or honey

2 tablespoons toasted sesame oil

BUTTERNUT SQUASH IN GREEN CURRY SAUCE

⤐ Serves 4 ⤏

My first introduction to Thai curries came while I assisted a friend in preparing a luncheon for Nancy Reagan at the Reagan Presidential Library in Simi Valley, California. What a surprise: the curry sauce was red! Although Thai curries have many ingredients in common with those of neighboring India, they tend to be tinged with a hint of sweetness from the combination of coconut milk and a traditional dash of sugar, and they are often colored red or green by the red or green chiles in them, rather than the more familiar yellow color of Indian curries. As with most Thai curries, serve this over rice.

Place the squash and water in the slow cooker insert. Cover and cook on low for 3 to 4 hours, or until the squash is tender when pierced with a fork.

In a blender, combine the onion, garlic, ginger, chile, $^1/_2$ cup of the cilantro, sugar, and coconut milk. Blend until it forms a smooth green paste, then add salt to taste.

Once the squash is tender, pour in the sauce and continue cooking just until heated through, 20 to 30 minutes.

Serve garnished with the remaining $^1/_4$ cup cilantro leaves and the Thai basil.

SUGGESTED BEVERAGE: A nice crisp, off-dry white wine would be lovely here.

1 butternut squash, peeled, seeded, and cut into 1-inch cubes (about 4 cups)

$^1/_2$ cup water

2 tablespoons chopped yellow onion

2 cloves garlic, peeled

1-inch piece fresh ginger, peeled and coarsely chopped

1 serrano chile, stemmed, seeded, and deveined

$^3/_4$ cup coarsely chopped cilantro leaves

1 teaspoon sugar

1 can (about 14 ounces) unsweetened coconut milk

Salt to taste

$^1/_4$ cup fresh Thai basil leaves, thinly sliced, for garnish (optional)

Japanese-Style Braised Tofu

≫ Serves 4 ≪

Even my meat-eating friends, quietly polite when invited to a dinner featuring tofu, rave about this one. It is easy and delicious and contains flavors traditionally considered typical of both Japanese- and Korean-style cooking. Serve over brown rice.

Combine the miso paste, tamari, sesame oil, water, and honey in a soup bowl or shallow dish.

Carefully coat each slice of tofu in the sauce and then lay it in the slow cooker insert, being careful not to break it. Pour the sauce over the top of the tofu.

Cover and cook on low for about 4 hours, or until the tofu is hot all the way through and saturated in sauce.

Just before serving, add the spinach to the slow cooker insert, cover, and cook for about 10 minutes more, or until the spinach is thoroughly wilted.

Carefully remove the spinach and slices of tofu from the slow cooker and place a few slices on each plate. Garnish with the sesame seeds and sliced green onion and serve hot.

SUGGESTED BEVERAGE: Some delicious, light, aromatic white like a Sauvignon Blanc or a Gewürztraminer would be nice. Or something with bubbles. Or the standard beer.

$1/4$ cup white miso paste

$1/4$ cup tamari or low-sodium soy sauce

2 tablespoons sesame oil

2 tablespoons water

1 tablespoon honey

1 pound extra-firm tofu, drained and cut into $1/2$-inch slices

$1/2$ pound fresh spinach leaves

2 tablespoons sesame seeds, toasted, for garnish

1 green onion, thinly sliced, for garnish

Italy

Cracked Wheat Berries with Honey and Ricotta 59

Risotto with Lentils 60

Polenta Lasagna with Tomato-Mushroom Sauce 63

Barley, Mushroom, and Onion Soup 65

Polenta gnocchi in tomato sauce 66

Tuscan White Beans with Sage and Garlic 69

Fonduta Piemontese 70

Red Wine and Cherry Risotto 71

Italy, like France and Greece, has a wonderful repertoire of hours-long, oven-baked dishes, many of them based, like all peasant cuisines, on grains, fruits, and vegetables. There are two Italian specialities in particular that lend themselves well to the slow cooker: polenta and risotto. Made the traditional way, both dishes require that the cook stand over the pot and watch, stirring fairly constantly for long periods of time, making sure the dish comes out smooth.

However, thanks to the gentle, even heating provided by the slow cooker, polenta can be put in the pot with an appropriate amount of water and walked away from for 6 to 7 hours. Maybe you'd like to stir it once or twice, but basically, it prepares itself. To my mind, polenta is such a versatile food that it can be eaten for breakfast, lunch, or dinner and sauced with any number of sweet or savory ingredients. Using it as a component in the Polenta Lasagna recipe is only one of many ways it can be served. Try using it as a breakfast cereal topped with milk and honey. Or try mounding it on a plate and topping it with some of the Tomato-Mushroom Sauce and freshly grated Parmesan cheese.

Risotto, too, when made the traditional way, takes careful watching. However, the slow cooker makes the preparation of risotto a snap. Place the rice and water in the slow cooker insert, set on low, and walk away for a couple of hours. Put your feet up. Have a glass of wine. Watch a movie. Come back and enjoy a delicious, nourishing plate of Risotto with Lentils.

Another of the slow cooker's strengths is the gentle melting of cheese and wine for fondue, as in the Fonduta Piemontese. And cleanup is a breeze.

WINE WITH ITALIAN FOOD

My first introduction to Italian wines came from master sommelier Edmund Osterland, the first American to qualify in France as a master sommelier. Ed was teaching a wine appreciation class in San Diego, and he hauled out a couple of northern Italian wines and juxtaposed them with a couple of the more familiar California wines. To my unschooled palate, the difference was amazing. The Italian wines were crisp and acidic and lower in alcohol than their American counterparts. I didn't like them very much. I wanted the heavier mouthfeel and slight sweetness to which I was accustomed. Then Ed explained that the Italian wines are made to go with food, rather than to be sipped or drunk on their own, as American wines are. The idea that wine and food might be made with the intention of consuming them in tandem was novel to me.

Italian wines, like those of any wine-producing region, have grown up alongside the foods of the region. Every little corner of this country produces wine, often from its own unique grape varieties, of which Italy has more than one thousand! (Dizzying thought to those of us brought up in the Cabernet-Chardonnay frame of reference.) To study them is to study the history of the people who have made and planted them.

In general, people seem to be most enthusiastic about the wines of northern Italy, and in particular those of Tuscany, Piedmont, and the northeastern regions of Friuli, Alto Adige, and Veneto. It is the wines from these regions that you are most likely to find in the United States, so you could begin your exploration and experimentation here. But I cannot resist saying that the best way to get a handle on Italian wines and their intimate relationship with Italian foods would be to pack your suitcase.

CRACKED WHEAT BERRIES WITH
HONEY AND RICOTTA

❧ Serves 3 to 4 ❧

Although most Americans are familiar with ground wheat hot breakfast cereals such as Wheatena, few of us would consider cracking whole wheat berries at home for breakfast. They are, however, aromatic and delicious, and eaten much like oatmeal (either whole or cracked) in some rural areas of Italy. This recipe works well in the 3-quart slow cooker that I use for risotto and polenta. Just put it on to cook at night before you go to bed and awaken to a delicious breakfast. Be sure to purchase "triple-cleaned" wheat from your health foods store or use a commercially prepared seven-grain cereal if you don't want to go to the trouble of cracking your own wheat.

Pulse the wheat berries briefly in your blender or food processor, just enough to crack them into pieces. Do not powder them.

Place the cracked wheat, water, and salt in the slow cooker insert. Cover and cook on low overnight, about 8 hours.

In the morning, dish up servings of cracked wheat, then top each with a scoop of ricotta cheese. Drizzle generously with honey, and then sprinkle with ground cinnamon and a dusting of cocoa powder.

SUGGESTED BEVERAGE: You could conceivably kick-start your day Italian style with some grappa in your coffee, but I'm thinking a nice espresso or cappuccino after breakfast would do the trick—and make focusing on the drive to work a whole lot safer.

1 cup hard wheat berries

4 cups water

$1/2$ teaspoon salt

$1^1/2$ cups fresh ricotta cheese

Honey

Ground cinnamon, for garnish

Cocoa powder or shaved
    semisweet chocolate,
    for garnish

RISOTTO WITH LENTILS

~ Serves 4 ~

Over many centuries, every country in the world has developed ways to obtain much-needed protein by combining the simplest of ingredients. In Italy, the combination of lentils and rice has found just as happy a home as it has in India. The trimmings may be a little different, but this simple dish can make a meal in itself when served with a salad, or as an accompaniment to grilled vegetables or stuffed artichokes.

Thoroughly rinse the lentils and rice, being sure to remove any small stones or dirt. Place them in the slow cooker insert along with the water and 1 teaspoon salt.

In a sauté pan, heat the butter and sauté the onion over medium-high heat until the onion is golden brown, about 10 minutes.

Add the onion to the lentils and rice. Cover and cook on high for about 2 hours, or until both the lentils and the rice are tender. Add additional salt, if necessary, and pepper to taste.

Top each serving with a drizzle of the olive oil and a generous sprinkling of the Parmesan cheese and the parsley.

SUGGESTED BEVERAGE: Any good, medium-bodied red wine would be nice with this dish. I might try a Barbera or a young, fruity Zinfandel or one of my favorite easy-drinking Italian varietals, Callaway Vineyards' Dolcetto.

1/2 cup dried lentils

3/4 cup Arborio rice

4 cups water

1 teaspoon salt, plus more to taste

2 tablespoons unsalted butter

1/2 yellow onion, chopped

Freshly ground black pepper to taste

1 tablespoon good, fruity olive oil

1/2 cup freshly grated Parmesan cheese

1/4 cup finely chopped fresh parsley, for garnish

POLENTA LASAGNA WITH
TOMATO-MUSHROOM SAUCE

~ Serves 4 to 6 ~

For most of us, the mention of lasagna conjures up mouthwatering images of rich tomato sauce layered with rich cheeses and thin noodles. But a type of lasagna can also be made using polenta rather than pasta. In this polenta lasagna, the old familiar formula appears, but the packaging (polenta instead of lasagna noodles) is new. I recommend making the tomato sauce a day ahead of time, and possibly having two slow cookers on hand so that you can pour the polenta quickly from one into the other.

To make the sauce, using a paring knife, cut a cross in the stem end of each tomato, then drop them into a pot of boiling water. When the skins begin to come loose, carefully remove the tomatoes from the water with a skimmer, allow them to cool slightly, and then peel off the skins. Chop the tomatoes very coarsely and place them in the insert of the slow cooker.

Rinse the dried mushrooms, then soak them in a small bowl in about 1 cup of water for 30 minutes. Lift out the softened mushrooms, leaving any grit behind, and squeeze the excess liquid out of them. Add the mushrooms to the tomatoes.

Heat the 2 tablespoons of oil in a skillet and sauté the onion until golden brown, 7 to 10 minutes. Add the garlic and sauté for about 1 minute longer, then add the mixture to the insert. Cover, and cook on low for 6 to 8 hours, or until the sauce has thickened to your liking. Stir in the remaining olive oil and season with salt and freshly ground pepper to taste. The sauce can be made a day ahead and kept refrigerated in a covered container.

To make the polenta, combine the polenta, water, and salt in a clean slow cooker insert. Cover and cook on low for about 6 hours, or until the polenta is creamy and the grains are tender. Stir once or twice during cooking.

(continued)

Tomato-Mushroom Sauce

4 pounds flavorful tomatoes

1 ounce dried porcini or cremini mushrooms

2 tablespoons plus 1/4 cup olive oil (preferably a high-quality, fruity olive oil)

1/2 yellow onion, finely chopped

6 cloves garlic, peeled and finely chopped

Salt and freshly ground black pepper to taste

Basic Polenta

1 cup polenta

5 cups water

1 teaspoon salt

While the polenta is cooking, prepare the lasagna.

To make the lasagna, oil the inside of a slow cooker insert (this is when having two slow cookers comes in handy!) and prepare and set out the other ingredients so assembly will be quick and easy.

In a large bowl, thoroughly combine the Parmesan, mozzarella, parsley, basil, nutmeg, and pepper using your clean hands. In a small bowl and using a garlic press, press the garlic into the ricotta cheese and mix thoroughly.

When the polenta is done cooking, pour half of it into the bottom of the oiled slow cooker insert, carefully smoothing it into a neat layer. Next, carefully pour 1 cup of the sauce over the polenta, trying not to disturb it. Sprinkle half of the Parmesan-mozzarella mixture over the sauce, and then drop balls of ricotta over the cheese, using *all* of the ricotta. Carefully spoon in the remainder of the polenta, trying not to disturb the cheese–tomato sauce layer, then top the layer of polenta with the remaining cheese.

Cover and cook on low for about 2 hours, or until all the cheese is melted and the casserole is hot all the way through.

Allow to set for about 15 minutes after turning off the slow cooker. The portions may not come out set as perfectly as they would from a regular lasagna pan, but the contents will be colorful and delicious. This is another one of those dishes that is just as good the day after!

SUGGESTED BEVERAGE: Anything, just as long as it is red and dry. I can think of all sorts of wines I would enjoy with this dish: California Zin, Barbera, Chianti Classico, or super Tuscan (when I can get it).

Lasagna

2 tablespoons olive oil

1/2 cup Parmesan cheese (freshly grated, if possible)

8 ounces mozzarella cheese, grated

1/4 cup finely chopped fresh parsley

6 large fresh basil leaves, rolled like a cigar, then thinly sliced into strips

1/4 teaspoon ground nutmeg

Freshly ground black pepper to taste

2 to 4 cloves garlic

1 cup ricotta cheese

BARLEY, MUSHROOM, AND ONION SOUP

∽ Serves 4 ∽

It's delicious. It's typical of the kind of peasant soup you might find in a mountainous region where barley grows plentifully, and mushrooms are to be had in season. And best of all, it's a put-the-stuff-in-the-pot-and-walk-away-from-it no-brainer.

Place the barley and water in the slow cooker insert.

In a sauté pan, heat the oil and sauté the onion until golden brown, about 10 minutes.

Rinse the dried mushrooms and then soak them in a small bowl in about a cup of water for 30 minutes. Lift out the softened mushrooms, leaving any grit behind, and squeeze the excess liquid out of them. Pour the soaking water through a strainer lined with a damp paper towel or a coffee filter. Coarsely chop the mushrooms.

Add the mushrooms and the strained soaking water, the sautéed onion, the tomato sauce, carrot, and celery to the barley. Cover and cook on low for 6 to 8 hours, or until the barley is completely tender. Add the parsley and salt and pepper to taste.

Serve sprinkled with a tablespoon or two of freshly grated Parmesan.

SUGGESTED BEVERAGE: Personally, I'd prefer a beer with this hearty, simple peasant soup.

1 cup pearl barley, rinsed thoroughly

8 cups water

2 tablespoons olive oil

1 onion, thinly sliced

$1/2$ ounce dried porcini mushrooms

2 tablespoons tomato sauce

$1/2$ cup diced carrot

1 cup diced celery

2 tablespoons chopped fresh parsley

Salt and freshly ground black pepper to taste

$1/2$ cup freshly grated Parmesan cheese

POLENTA GNOCCHI IN TOMATO SAUCE

You can serve polenta in its most traditional form, but you can also use it to create an easy variation on gnocchi. I first learned this technique from my friend, Milan-born and -raised cooking teacher Nadia Frigieri. Making both the polenta and the sauce in a slow cooker means there's little hands-on effort required to make this stunning dish. Adding a green salad makes this a meal.

Prepare a baking sheet by placing a layer of aluminum foil over the surface, then grease with half of the olive oil.

Spread the just-cooked polenta in a smooth layer on the baking sheet and refrigerate the polenta until cool and firm, 2 to 4 hours. Use a biscuit or ravioli cutter to stamp out rounds of polenta.

Preheat the oven to 400°F. Prepare a baking dish by coating it with the remaining olive oil. Arrange the polenta gnocchi so the pieces are slightly overlapping one another in the bottom of the baking dish. Generously spoon the sauce over the polenta gnocchi and bake until hot, about 30 minutes.

Remove the gnocchi from the oven and sprinkle with the Parmesan and parsley, then grind some fresh pepper over the top. Serve immediately.

SUGGESTED BEVERAGE: A medium- to full-bodied red wine, such as a Sangiovese, super Tuscan, or a Zinfandel, would be a good choice.

$1/4$ cup olive oil

1 recipe Basic Polenta (page 63)

1 recipe Tomato-Mushroom Sauce (page 63)

$1/4$ cup freshly grated Parmesan cheese

$1/4$ cup finely chopped fresh parsley, for garnish

Freshly ground black pepper

Tuscan White Beans with Sage and Garlic

Beans are as much a staple in Tuscany as they are in rural regions anyplace else in the world. Traditionally cooked in an earthenware pot called a fagioliera, *this simple bean dish works beautifully in a slow cooker insert. Embellish it with fresh vegetables such as tomatoes or summer squash if you like, then serve with a crusty loaf of French bread and a green salad. Choosing good-quality salt and olive oil will help elevate the dish to something special.*

Wash the beans thoroughly, then put them, along with the water, bay leaves, and sage sprigs in the slow cooker insert. Leave the head of garlic whole, wrap it in cheesecloth if desired, and add to the beans. Cover and cook on low for 6 to 8 hours, or until the beans are tender.

Remove the garlic and herbs from the beans, then add salt to taste and a pinch of red pepper flakes. Stir in the olive oil.

Ladle individual servings into bowls and garnish each with a fresh sage leaf or two.

SUGGESTED BEVERAGE: I personally would enjoy this simple meal with a hearty red Tuscan (or super Tuscan) wine. I'm not picky. I like most all of them!

2 cups dried cannellini beans

6 cups water

2 bay leaves

2 sprigs sage, plus extra leaves for garnish

1 head garlic

Salt to taste

Pinch of red pepper flakes (optional)

$1/3$ cup extra-virgin olive oil

FONDUTA PIEMONTESE

~~ Serves 4 ~~

Fondue has provided nourishment to mountain folk in Switzerland and the Italian and French Alps through many a hard, cold winter. Made from what must have been, at times, the only ingredients at hand, stale bread and hard cheese, the communal rites that developed around the eating of fondue sustained spirits as well as bodies. Although Emmentaler, Gruyère, and fontina are fondue classics, you can actually use any kind of "mountain" cheese, such as Appenzeller, Comté, or Beaufort. The slow, even heat of the slow cooker is just perfect for making a smooth, effortless fondue. I suggest using a 2- or 3-quart slow cooker for the fondue. It fits more easily on the table and is a more suitable size for this amount of fondue.

In a plastic bag, combine the cheese and cornstarch and shake until the cheese is coated with cornstarch.

Place the cheese-cornstarch mixture, the white wine, and the garlic in the slow cooker insert. Cover and heat on low for about 2 hours, stirring occasionally, until the cheese is thoroughly melted and the mixture has thickened. Add a dash of nutmeg.

You can then transfer the fondue mixture to a fondue pot and place it on the table, or you can place the slow cooker on the table and allow people to dip in with the bread cubes speared on skewers.

SUGGESTED BEVERAGE: A dry northern Italian white such as a Pinot Grigio or Cortese would work nicely here. I also think I might enjoy a Nebbiolo or a Barolo.

16 ounces cheese, cubed (single variety or a combination; see headnote)

1 1/2 tablespoons cornstarch

1 cup dry white wine

1 clove garlic

Dash of freshly ground nutmeg

1 loaf rustic country bread, cut into 1-inch cubes

RED WINE AND CHERRY RISOTTO

❧ Serves 4 ❧

Although this unusual risotto could be served with Parmesan cheese shaved over the top as a savory side dish, it's at its best as a dessert. Serve it warm and topped off with a scoop of vanilla ice cream or some sweetened whipped cream. Gobble it all up before the ice cream has a chance to melt.

Rinse the rice thoroughly, then place the rice, butter, wine, water, and cherries in the slow cooker insert.

Cover and cook on high for about 2 hours, or until the rice is tender and the liquid absorbed.

Remove the cover and stir in the cream. Serve warm.

SUGGESTED BEVERAGE: I, personally, wouldn't drink wine with this dish, but would prefer to savor every bite, then follow it with an espresso. However, dessert or ice wine might complement the dish if you'd like to try it.

1 cup Arborio rice

2 tablespoons butter

2 cups dry, fruity red wine

2 cups water

4 ounces dried, pitted tart cherries

1/4 cup heavy cream or half-and-half

France

I remember my first French cooking vessel: an earthenware casserole from Vallauris, purchased at Williams-Sonoma when the only Williams-Sonoma in the world was located in downtown San Francisco. It was recommended by Julia Child as being an excellent vessel for making French stews and casseroles, and I just had to have one. The first meal I made in it came from *Mastering the Art of French Cooking*—a *boeuf bourguignon*, the quintessential French one-pot meal.

Since that time, I have been fascinated by the plethora of French casseroles and dishes that lend themselves so well to the long, slow cook. Many were born of centuries of using similar earthenware vessels baked in a communal oven. (To save fuel and time, many villages had what they called a *four banale*, or common oven, an oven that everyone in the village could use, so that fuel was not wasted in myriad individual homes.)

Many such dishes contained meat, but many, of necessity, as with all cultures around the world, were made of vegetables in season, at times perhaps seasoned with a hint of meat, but more often with aromatic herbs and vegetables that could be gathered in the surrounding hillsides.

I can envision the French Alpine Cheese, Tomato, and Onion Soup, for instance, bubbling away on a stove top for hours, filling the air with the smells of a summer evening in the Alps. Or the Smoky Potage Saint-Germain, with its simple, hearty base of split peas, sending its earthy, smoky fragrance wafting into the air on a cold winter afternoon. And while

I'm not likely to concoct a classic *boeuf bourguignon* these days, I have not given up the wine that so enriches it. On the contrary, I've tossed it into a pot of beans.

WINES WITH FRENCH FOOD

For many of us, French wines served as the door through which we passed into the world of wine. And for many of us, French wines were the yardstick against which we measured wine quality. Winemaking in France has a long and venerable history, going back to the earliest days of the Roman occupation, and probably going back to primitive efforts to ferment wild grapes of the region long before that.

Who doesn't know the names of France's major wine-producing regions and the unique wines that have been made there for centuries—the elegant Pinot Noirs of Burgundy, the crisp whites of the Loire Valley, the rich, inky reds of the southern Rhône, the aromatic whites of Alsace, the imperial reds and whites of the Bordeaux region, and the most spectacular sparkling wines in the world from the Champagne region? Then there are the more rustic but equally interesting wines from more obscure regions: Languedoc-Roussillon, Côtes de Provence, the Jura Mountains, Côtes de Ventoux, and so on.

This is a country in which, like Italy, wines and food have grown up together. The wines are made to accompany food and the foods are made to be consumed with wine. Get a wine map and explore. First from your armchair, then eventually, by exploring France's wine regions and their foods on the ground, because all wines should ultimately be sampled in their natural environs.

French Alpine Cheese, Tomato, and Onion Soup

⤳ Serves 4 ⤳

One of the great joys of my childhood was having my mother read to me from Heidi. *Heidi drank goat's milk from a bowl for breakfast and had soup for dinner. In the Swiss Alps, Heidi enjoyed a feast that has sustained and nurtured people the world over for many centuries: soups, sometimes featuring the simplest of ingredients (as simple as some oats or flour, a nip of onion, and some broth or milk). Soups like this one have been made and drunk in France's mountainous regions for breakfast, lunch, and dinner. All you need are some really flavorful ingredients, a creative mind, and a loving heart. Note: Don't buy hard, flavorless tomatoes in the dead of winter and expect this simple soup to taste good! Use the best, freshest tomatoes you can find, preferably from your own garden, picked at the peak of ripeness on a late summer's day. This is not a winter soup.*

In a large sauté pan, heat the oil and butter and sauté the onions over medium-high heat until golden brown, about 10 minutes. (I find it easiest to do this in two batches.)

Salt the onions lightly, then sprinkle them with the flour and place them in the slow cooker insert. Add the tomatoes, wine, and water. Cover and cook on low for 6 to 8 hours, or until the onions are quite soft and flavors have had a chance to meld.

When you are ready to serve the soup, adjust the salt to your taste, place a slice or so of bread in the bottom of each soup bowl, then toss in some of the cheese. Ladle some hot soup and vegetables over the top of the bread and cheese and serve.

SUGGESTED BEVERAGE: I would enjoy either a dry, acidic white wine such as an Alsatian Pinot Gris or Riesling, or a good, fruity mountain red.

2 tablespoons vegetable oil

2 tablespoons unsalted butter

2 yellow onions, thinly sliced

Salt to taste (I use both smoked and sea salt)

$1/3$ cup all-purpose flour

2 pounds tomatoes, coarsely chopped

$1/2$ cup dry white wine

6 cups water

4 to 6 slices country bread, well toasted

$1/2$ pound Gruyère or Tomme de Savoie cheese, diced (about 1 cup)

Cold Provençal White Bean Salad

⤳ Serves 6 to 8 ⤳

One of the things I enjoyed most on my first visits to France were the cold rice and bean salads. They seemed so simple, and the only rice and beans I had eaten at home were hot and served in soups or casseroles, or under some creamed meat. Here is a typical French-style cold white bean salad.

Thoroughly rinse the beans and place them and the water in the slow cooker insert. Cover and cook on low for 6 to 8 hours, or until the beans are tender. Quickly and gently pour them into a colander and drain them. (You can reserve the cooking water and use it to thicken soups or stews.) Transfer the beans to a serving bowl.

In a small bowl, combine the vinegar, oil, mustard, and garlic. Blend thoroughly with a whisk or an immersion blender.

Pour the dressing over the beans and mix thoroughly. Add the green onions, olives, and salt and pepper to taste, and toss by hand (or if you must, using spoons).

Serve either chilled or at room temperature on lettuce leaves and garnish with the tomato wedges.

SUGGESTED BEVERAGE: A chilled Tavel rosé would be nice.

2 cups dried small white beans

6 cups water

1/4 cup white wine vinegar

1/2 cup olive oil

2 tablespoons Dijon mustard

2 cloves garlic, pressed

4 green onions, green part only, very thinly sliced

1 cup Mediterranean-style olives, pitted and halved

Salt and freshly ground black pepper to taste

6 to 8 large lettuce leaves

2 small tomatoes, cut into wedges, for garnish

Scalloped Potatoes Auvergnats

∽ Serves 4 to 6 ∽

Few countries do potatoes and cheese as well as France and Switzerland. Raclette, scalloped potatoes, pommes de terre dauphinoises, *whipped, or whatever, a couple hundred years of potatoes and cheese and a knack for cooking have made them experts at the many comforting ways these two inexpensive, favorite ingredients can be combined. The Auvergne is a region in south–central France known, among other things, for its popular blue cheese called Bleu d'Auvergne.*

Arrange a layer of potatoes in the bottom of the slow cooker insert, then sprinkle about 2 teaspoons flour and $^1/_4$ teaspoon salt evenly over the layer. Place several small dots of butter on the layer. Then sprinkle on a tablespoon or two of cheese.

Repeat, adding layers of potatoes topped with flour, salt, butter, and cheese, until all the potatoes have been used up. (One large potato yields about one layer.) End with a plain layer of potatoes, but save a bit of cheese for a final layer later. Cover and cook on low for about 3 hours.

Remove the lid, pour the milk over all, top with a last layer of cheese, recover, and cook for 1 to 3 hours longer, or until all the potatoes are tender. Do not be afraid to stir the potatoes very gently as they are cooking. When you spoon them out of the insert they will become disarranged—no matter how carefully you have arranged them to start with—and a gentle stir will keep all the good stuff evenly distributed and help disguise any graying of potatoes that are exposed to oxygen.

Let the potatoes rest for 10 minutes, and then scoop large spoonfuls onto plates.

Variations: Some of my favorite variations on the theme of scalloped potatoes and cheese are sharp cheddar and chives, Gruyère and freshly grated nutmeg, and smoked cheddar and fresh parsley.

SUGGESTED BEVERAGE: Perhaps a good, hearty red wine from southwestern France would be nice. A tannic Minervois? A dry rosé? Almost anything that you would pair with a blue cheese would work well here.

3 or 4 russet potatoes, peeled and sliced $^1/_4$ inch thick

$^1/_4$ cup all-purpose flour

Salt to taste

2 tablespoons unsalted butter

$^1/_4$ pound Bleu d'Auvergne, Stilton, Roquefort, or domestic blue cheese, grated, thinly sliced, or crumbled

$1^1/_2$ cups milk or half-and-half

SMOKY POTAGE SAINT-GERMAIN

≈ Serves 4 to 6 ≈

Most split pea soup recipes are ridiculously predictable. Some onion, a bit of carrot, maybe some cut-up spuds. A ham hock. Inevitably, split peas are the main attraction, usually cooked to a mushy consistency. But I was looking for texture and additional flavor, so I added some dried chanterelle mushrooms; half an onion, thinly sliced and well browned; some chopped tomatoes; fresh celery leaves; carrots; and spinach. I considered adding liquid smoke because the ham hock was out. But as luck would have it, one of my wooden spoons caught on fire, so I let it burn, then put out the fire and stuck the charred spoon in the soup. If a winemaker can use charred oak to enhance the flavors of her wine, then why can't I use charred wood for that desired essence of smoke in my soup? (P.S. DO NOT try this at home! Using a smoked salt should achieve similar effects without the fire!)

Place the split peas, water, and mushrooms in the slow cooker insert.

In a skillet, heat the oil and sauté the onion over medium-high heat until golden brown, about 10 minutes. Add the onion, celery leaves, tomatoes, and carrots to the split peas. Cover and cook for 6 to 8 hours, or until the split peas are tender.

About 15 minutes before serving, add the spinach leaves and season with smoked salt to taste. Serve piping hot.

SUGGESTED BEVERAGE: A classic beverage for drinking with Smoky Potage Saint-Germain is beer rather than wine.

2 cups dried split peas, washed

8 cups water

1/2 ounce dried chanterelles or other mushrooms, rinsed well

1 tablespoon olive or vegetable oil

1 yellow or red onion, thinly sliced

1/4 cup chopped celery leaves

1/2 cup chopped fresh tomatoes

1/4 cup thinly sliced carrots

1 cup fresh spinach leaves

Smoked salt to taste

Egg, Cheese, and Onion Quiche

∽ Serves 4 to 6 ∽

A classic quiche Lorraine has long been one of my favorite dishes. You can make a good crustless, meatless version in the slow cooker, drawing upon that gentle heat. I like to use a smoked salt to supply the smoky flavor that bacon would ordinarily give. Serve with a crispy green salad.

In a large sauté pan, heat the oil and sauté the onion until wilted and starting to brown, 5 to 7 minutes. Add the mushrooms and continue to sauté until both the onion and the mushrooms are golden brown, 5 to 7 minutes more. Add the smoked salt and pepper to taste.

Spread the bread crumbs evenly over the bottom of the slow cooker insert. Using a slotted spoon so any excess moisture can drain off, carefully spread the sautéed mushrooms and onion on top of the bread crumbs, being careful not to displace the layer of bread crumbs. Spread the cheese in a single layer on top of the mushrooms and onions.

In a blender or food processor, combine the eggs, a dash of salt, the sour cream, and the nutmeg until thoroughly blended.

Gently pour the egg mixture over the contents of the slow cooker insert. Cover and cook on low for 2 to 3 hours, or until the center still jiggles slightly but is just about set. (Always stop the cooking *before* the quiche is completely set. If you wait until the top is set, the quiche is likely to be dry and overcooked.)

Serve by carefully spooning a generous portion of the quiche out of the slow cooker insert and onto plates or shallow bowls.

Variation: For a nontraditional "americanized" crust, try spreading a cup or two of grated potatoes evenly over the bottom of a well-oiled or buttered slow cooker insert, then proceeding with the recipe above.

SUGGESTED BEVERAGE: An Alsatian Pinot Gris or other nice light, dry white wine would be nice. I think I'd just as well enjoy a sparkling wine, Prosecco, or champagne, too.

2 tablespoons vegetable oil

1 onion, cut in half and thinly sliced

8 ounces fresh mushrooms, sliced

Smoked salt to taste

Freshly ground black pepper to taste

1 cup toasted bread crumbs

1 cup (about 1/4 pound) grated Gruyère or Swiss cheese

6 large eggs

1 cup sour cream

Pinch of freshly grated nutmeg

Uncle Bob's Green Lentil Salad

❧ Serves 6 to 8 ❧

My uncle Bob, an artist and a designer, has lived in Paris most of his adult life. The last time I visited him, he took me to a small, favorite bistro near his atelier in the 14th arrondissement. We began our meal with a simple, cold green lentil salad, a popular appetizer all over France.

Rinse the lentils thoroughly, being sure to remove any small stones or dirt. Place them in the slow cooker insert along with water to cover by 2 inches. Cover and cook on low for about 2 hours, or until the lentils are tender but still have texture. They should be al dente, so do not overcook them or they will turn to mush. Drain the lentils.

In a small bowl, whisk together the oil and vinegar, and add salt and pepper to taste. Press the garlic into the dressing and mix thoroughly.

Mix the dressing thoroughly into the lentils while they are still warm, then top with the finely chopped onion.

Serve at room temperature.

SUGGESTED BEVERAGE: I think I would enjoy a lively Pinot Noir with this dish (or all by itself, for that matter).

2 cups dried French green lentils

Water

2 tablespoons olive oil

$1/4$ cup red wine vinegar

Salt and freshly ground black pepper to taste

1 clove garlic

$1/2$ onion, finely chopped

STEAMED ARTICHOKES

⤳ Serves 2 to 3 ⤳

"What's the advantage to cooking artichokes in a slow cooker?" you might ask. The answer is that while the arti-chokes are cooking, you've bought yourself a big chunk of time to do other things while the chokes cook completely unattended. If you are like me, you may get no further than pulling the chokes out of the pot with tongs and sitting down to them with a nice serving of homemade garlic-tarragon mayo. But I've given a few other suggestions in case you get bored.

Trim the stems off the artichokes and strip off any extra leaves. Using a very sharp knife, carefully cut off a generous one-third at the top of each artichoke. This will remove most of the thorns and expose the center of the artichoke.

Rinse the chokes thoroughly, then arrange them in the slow cooker insert (an oval-shaped cooker works best). Pour in the water, cover, and cook on low for about 6 hours, or until a fork easily pierces the stem end of the choke or a leaf can easily be pulled off.

Meanwhile, prepare the stuffing or mayo.

To make the stuffing, break up the bread slices and put them in the bowl of a food processor. Pulse until the bread is in large crumbs. Add the parsley, garlic, tomato, lemon juice, olive oil, and salt to taste and pulse until thoroughly mixed.

To make the mayo, place the vinegar, egg, and mustard in the bowl of a food processor or a blender and mix thoroughly. With the machine running, drop in the garlic cloves, then slowly pour in the vegetable oil. Pouring the oil slowly is important to the process of thickening the mayo. When the mayo has thickened, drop in the tarragon and pulse just until thoroughly mixed in. (If you let the machine continue to run, you will have green mayo, which, in some cases, might be just the ticket.) Add salt and freshly ground pepper to taste.

(continued)

3 medium or 2 large artichokes (or however many will fit in the insert of your slow cooker)

4 cups water

Stuffing (optional)

4 slices country bread, dried out

$1/4$ cup coarsely chopped fresh parsley

2 cloves garlic, finely minced

1 Roma tomato, minced

1 teaspoon fresh lemon juice

2 to 3 tablespoons olive oil

Salt to taste

Garlic-Tarragon Mayo

1 tablespoon white wine, sherry, or apple cider vinegar

1 egg

1 teaspoon Dijon mustard

4 or more cloves garlic, peeled and smashed with a knife

$1^1/2$ cups vegetable oil

1 to 2 tablespoons chopped fresh tarragon leaves

Salt and freshly ground black pepper to taste

Carefully remove the artichokes from the water using tongs and invert them in a colander or strainer so that any excess water can drain out. Using a spoon or your fingers, pull out the fuzzy center choke of each artichoke, leaving a nice hole. (It is important to let the artichokes cool somewhat before attempting to remove the chokes so that you do not burn your fingers.)

If you are using the stuffing, spoon some of the stuffing into each cavity. Spoon the mayo into small bowls for dipping.

Serve warm or at room temperature. (Unstuffed artichokes can be eaten even cold.)

Note: For some fun and entertainment at your next party, give several guests a large mortar and pestle and the ingredients for the mayo and let them make the mayo by hand. Put the vinegar, egg, mustard, and garlic in the mortar and smash it up. Incorporate the vegetable oil a few drops at a time, pounding it in with the pestle, until the mayo is nice and thick. Be sure to keep their wineglasses full!

SUGGESTED BEVERAGE: Artichokes are generally considered a difficult food to pair with wines. I think the fun would be to experiment and find out what, if anything, works. Put out some bottles of rosé, a chilled white or two (Gewürztraminer, Pinot Gris, or Grigio), perhaps a sparkling wine, and maybe even a red.

WALNUT AND APPLE BREAD PUDDING

∾ Serves 4 to 6 ∾

Apples and walnuts ripen at about the same time, and are often grown in the same region. Pair them with a crusty, rustic loaf of bread, some spices, milk, and eggs, and you've got a perfect dessert for a fall afternoon. Puddings and bread puddings are particularly easy to make in a slow cooker, and the results are nearly always perfect.

Coat the interior of the slow cooker insert with the butter.

In a large mixing bowl, combine the bread, apples, cinnamon, walnuts, and raisins and mix them together as thoroughly as possible. (I use clean hands, the best mixing device I know of.) Place the bread and apple mixture in the slow cooker insert.

In a blender, combine the milk, sugar, and eggs and blend thoroughly. Gently pour the liquid over the bread, using a spoon to press the bread down into the liquid.

Cover and cook on low for about 3 hours, or until the liquid has been absorbed by the bread and a crust is beginning to form.

Turn off the slow cooker and allow the pudding to settle for 15 to 20 minutes, then spoon individual portions into bowls and top each portion with a generous serving of whipped cream and a sprinkling of brown sugar.

SUGGESTED BEVERAGE: Tea or coffee are good choices here. If you can find one, a Canadian apple ice wine would be delightful.

2 tablespoons unsalted butter

6 cups levain or country bread, cut into 1-inch cubes

2 Granny Smith apples, peeled, cored, and cut into 1-inch (or smaller) cubes

2 tablespoons ground cinnamon or apple pie spice

1 cup chopped walnuts

$1/2$ cup raisins

4 cups whole milk

$1/2$ cup sugar

4 large eggs

Whipped cream or ice cream, for serving

Brown sugar, for sprinkling

Greece

Like the rustic cooking of all countries, Greek cuisine reflects the many peoples and cultures that have passed through and contributed to making this beautiful country what it is today. And just as rustic dishes may vary greatly from one region of a country to another, so do those of Greece.

For most Americans, Greek food consists of a very limited repertoire of delicious dishes: cured olives, hummus, *melitzanosalata* (mashed eggplant) and feta cheese, moussaka, pastitsio, avgolemono (lemon-flavored chicken soup), and the ubiquitous "Greek salad." But what few of us realize is that what passes for "Greek food" here in the United States is but a very narrow spectrum of the cuisine of the country as a whole.

What most Americans recognize as Greek food has its origins in the islands and the coastal mainland of southern Greece. Travel inland and north and you find a very different culture, architecture, people, and, of course, rustic cuisine.

For instance, Stuffed Peppers Florina makes use of one of Macedonia's (the mountainous region of northern Greece, which the Greeks claim is the true Macedonia of Alexander the Great) most well-known agricultural products: peppers. As Greece-born food writer Diane Kolchilas says, "Peppers are to Macedonia what corn is to Kansas."

WINES WITH GREEK FOOD

You may be scratching your head wondering where to find a Greek wine. And if you do find it, will it be any good? For many of us, our only exposure to Greek wine has been the poor-quality, piney-tasting retsina we may have tried at a Greek restaurant, on a Greek island, or at a Greek Orthodox church festival. Few of us have had any exposure to the wonderful and unique wines coming out of Greece today.

I have a number of terrific Greek wines in my small personal collection, and I would like to encourage you to seek out and try the new generation of wines from boutique winemakers in Greece. Many of Greece's most talented winemakers today have studied winemaking in Bordeaux, California, or Australia. Not only are they growing and making wines from the noble grape varieties with which we are all familiar, but they are also applying cutting-edge European and New World winemaking techniques to their unique repertoire of indigenous Greek grape varieties. Most of these varieties have names that will be difficult for you to pronounce, but believe me when I say that a whole new world of flavors and aromas awaits you in well-made Greek wines. Because of the growing popularity of Greek wines, they are becoming easier to find in American wine shops and markets. I can highly recommend the wines of Kir-Yianni Estate, Gaia Estate, Alpha Estate, Boutari-Matsa Estate, and Château Geravassiliou, to name just a few.

GREEK-STYLE FAVA BEANS AND TOMATOES

❧ Serves 6 to 8 ❧

Countries all around the world make use of dried beans, and cook them, of necessity, in an oven or on a stove top for a long time, often dressing them in the simplest of ways. The Greeks, who serve them both as a meze (appetizer) and as a main dish, are no exception. For this dish, I've recommended fava beans, commonly used in Mediterranean countries, but Greeks often use a large, white bean called gigandas that can sometimes be found in Middle Eastern markets. Note: If you are using favas, be sure to buy blanched, skinless beans, as favas come encased in a tough, brownish shell and are sometimes sold that way. This dish makes a nice meal with a green salad and a crusty country loaf.

Rinse the beans thoroughly, removing any dirt or stones, then place them in the slow cooker insert along with the water. Cover and cook on low for 6 to 8 hours, or until the beans are nice and tender.

While the beans are cooking, heat 2 tablespoons of the oil in a sauté pan and sauté the onion until lightly browned, about 7 minutes. Add the tomatoes, bay leaves, and thyme to the pan and cook briefly.

Drain the beans and toss them with the tomato-onion mixture. Using a garlic press, press the garlic into the beans, and add the remaining 4 tablespoons olive oil and the lemon juice. Add salt and pepper to taste.

Serve hot or warm.

SUGGESTED BEVERAGE: I'd probably enjoy a retsina with this dish, or a Greek rosé.

2 cups dried fava beans or other large, white beans

7 cups water

6 tablespoons olive oil

1 onion, coarsely chopped

2 large tomatoes, coarsely chopped

2 bay leaves

2 sprigs fresh thyme

6 cloves garlic, peeled

2 tablespoons fresh lemon juice

Salt and freshly ground black pepper to taste

STUFFED GREEK ONIONS

∽ Serves 4 ∽

Stuffed eggplant, tomatoes, zucchini, and, in this case, onions typically make their appearance on the table for special occasions in traditional Greek homes. Vidalia onions, if you can find them, are a bit flatter and sweeter than yellow onions, and they are perfect for stuffing. Just slice a bit off the top and a tad off the bottom, and you've got the perfect "cup" for holding something delicious. Serve these with a plate of tomatoes or a green salad.

Using a sharp knife, slice about one-third off the top of each onion, leaving a flat crown. Then remove a small slice from the bottom so it will remain upright in the slow cooker. Using a grapefruit knife or melon baller, carefully scrape out as much of the onion's core as you can without ruining the onion. Place the onions in the slow cooker insert, pour in the water, cover, and cook on low for about 3 hours, or until the onions are somewhat tender when pierced with a paring knife.

While the onions are cooking, combine the cheeses, olive oil, currants, chopped mint, and pine nuts in a bowl, mix together with a fork, and add a pinch of freshly ground pepper. Remove the cover of the slow cooker and fill each onion with 2 to 3 tablespoons of the mixture.

Recover and continue cooking for about 1 hour longer, or until the cheeses are melted and the onions are very tender and getting brown around the edges. Spoon any liquid in the bottom of the cooker over the onions.

Garnish each onion with a sprig of fresh mint and serve either hot or at room temperature.

SUGGESTED BEVERAGE: Okay, I can't resist. I'd like to suggest a well-chilled glass of retsina with this dish. Even the cheap, generic stuff would do, and probably bring back fond memories of the Greek islands. But several of Greece's new generation of winemakers have experimented with making artisanal retsina, and I'd like to suggest that if you can find one, you buy it and drink it. Gaia Estates' Thalassitis is one I can happily recommend.

4 Vidalia or yellow onions, peeled

1 cup water

1/2 cup chèvre

1/2 cup feta cheese

2 tablespoons olive oil

2 tablespoons currants

1 tablespoon chopped fresh mint leaves

2 tablespoons pine nuts

Freshly ground black pepper to taste

Several sprigs fresh mint, for garnish

Greek Lemon, Artichoke, and Egg Soup

⮞ Serves 4 to 6 ⮜

This classic Greek soup is one of my favorites when I want to "lighten up" from a gustatory standpoint. It makes the perfect chicken soup substitute when you are just not feeling up to snuff, or a good light dinner when you've had enough of the restaurant-and-fine-dining circuit. It is traditionally made with chicken broth and small bits of chicken, but I think the meatless version yields even truer, clearer flavors. A touch of ground cumin adds yet another dimension to the flavor.

Rinse the rice thoroughly and place it, along with the water, in the slow cooker insert.

In a sauté pan, heat the oil and sauté the onion, celery, and artichokes over medium-high heat until just beginning to brown, about 7 minutes.

Add the vegetables to the water and rice, cover, and cook on low for 4 to 5 hours, or until the rice is tender. Add the cumin and 1/4 cup of the parsley to the soup.

In a medium bowl and using a whisk or a handheld immersion blender, beat the eggs and lemon juice together until frothy. Slowly add 2 ladles of broth, 1 ladle at a time, stirring constantly, to the lemon and egg mixture.

Add the lemon and broth mixture back into the soup, stirring constantly, and continue cooking for about 10 minutes more, or until heated through and beginning to thicken. (If you allow the soup to boil, the eggs will curdle.)

Add salt and pepper to taste, ladle into bowls, garnish with the remaining 1/4 cup parsley, and serve immediately.

SUGGESTED BEVERAGE: A nice Sauvignon Blanc or an artisanal Greek retsina, if you can find one, would pair well with this soup.

1/2 cup basmati or long-grain rice

6 cups water

1/4 cup olive oil

1/4 cup finely chopped onion

1/2 cup diced celery (leaves and stalks)

1 (12-ounce) package frozen artichokes, thawed, or 1 (14-ounce) can artichoke hearts

Pinch of ground cumin

1/2 cup chopped fresh parsley

2 large eggs

1/2 cup fresh lemon juice

Salt and freshly ground black pepper to taste

POTATO, ARTICHOKE, AND MUSHROOM STEW WITH KALAMATA OLIVES

≈ Serves 4 to 6 ≈

The ingredients in this simple vegetable stew are made to order for the long, slow heat of the communal oven or the slow cooker. Flavors meld, juices blend together, and the whole thing is a fragrant, pleasurable afternoon's work.

Rinse the dried mushrooms, then soak them in a small bowl in about 1 cup of water for 30 minutes. Lift out the softened mushrooms, leaving any grit behind, and squeeze the excess liquid out of them.

Wash the potatoes thoroughly. If they are large, halve or quarter them. Add the potatoes, mushrooms, artichoke hearts, garlic, wine, and tomato sauce to the slow cooker insert.

Cover and cook on low for 6 to 8 hours, or until the potatoes are tender and the flavors are blended. About 30 minutes before serving, add the olives, olive oil, and salt and pepper to taste.

Serve in a bowl garnished with the chopped rosemary.

SUGGESTED BEVERAGE: Try a glass of northern Greece's signature grape variety, Xinomavro, if you can find it, or Kir-Yianni's Akakies, a delicious Greek rosé.

1/2 ounce dried porcini mushrooms

3 pounds small red or white rose potatoes

1 (12-ounce) package frozen artichoke hearts or 1 (14-ounce) can artichoke hearts

2 cloves garlic, minced

1/2 cup dry white wine

2 cups Tomato-Mushroom Sauce (page 63)

1 cup Kalamata olives, pitted

1/4 cup olive oil

Salt and freshly ground black pepper to taste

1 teaspoon finely chopped fresh rosemary or basil

STUFFED PEPPERS FLORINA

⤚ Serves 4 to 6 ⤙

Florina peppers are named for a city in western Macedonia (Greece), a part of the Greek countryside in which peppers are an all-important agricultural crop. They have a thick, red, sweet, firm flesh and are perfect for stuffing. I was first served them at the table of Mrs. Fany Boutari, the gracious matriarch of Greece's premier winemaking family. While Florina peppers are not easily found in the United States, you can buy them roasted and bottled, or you may be lucky enough to find some red Anaheim chiles that will work. In a pinch, you can use good old green Anaheims or the bigger poblanos, as I do. They won't be quite as sweet, but they will be good.

To roast the chiles, place them on a baking sheet lined with aluminum foil about 8 inches from the broiler. Broil them until the skin blisters and turns black on both sides. (Do not burn the chiles themselves.) Remove the baking sheet from the oven and quickly cover the chiles with a clean dish towel. Let them sit, covered, until they are cool. Using a paring knife or your fingers, carefully peel off the skins, then slit one side and remove the seeds and veins.

In a bowl, combine the onion, rice, cinnamon, cumin, currants, dill, and parsley and mix thoroughly with a fork. Using a garlic press, press the garlic into the rice mixture. Add salt to taste and mix well.

Oil the slow cooker insert with the olive oil.

Fill each pepper with as much of the rice mixture as it will hold, then carefully put the chile back together and lay it in the bottom of the slow cooker insert.

When all the chiles are in the slow cooker, sprinkle them with the feta cheese, cover, and cook on low for about 2 hours, or until the chiles are tender and the stuffing is hot all the way through.

Tip: I often make a double batch of the stuffing and then freeze half of it in a plastic bag. That way, it is available for instant stuffed veggies (it works in eggplant, tomatoes, and zucchini). Use within a month or two.

SUGGESTED BEVERAGE: Three Rs: retsina, rosé, or red.

4 to 6 red or green fresh Anaheim or poblano chiles

$1/4$ onion, finely chopped

2 cups cooked rice

$1/2$ teaspoon ground cinnamon

$1/2$ teaspoon ground cumin

$1/3$ cup currants

2 tablespoons chopped fresh dill

$1/4$ cup chopped fresh parsley

2 cloves garlic

Salt to taste

3 tablespoons olive oil

$1/4$ cup crumbled feta cheese (optional)

Moussaka with Artichokes, Tomatoes, and Potatoes

❧ Serves 4 to 6 ❧

Moussaka is a quintessential Greek dish, and one that every American knows. Usually a delicious dish of layered eggplant, ground beef or lamb, tomatoes, onions, and, best of all, a thick custard topping, moussaka is one of my personal favorites. This version calls for only vegetables, a not-uncommon variation found in rural Greece. It does well in the slow cooker, but may be just a bit juicier than if baked in an open casserole dish in the oven.

Layer the potatoes in the bottom of the slow cooker insert. Then layer all the eggplant slices on top.

Grind the cinnamon, cloves, peppercorns, and allspice to a powder in an electric coffee mill or a mortar and pestle.

In a large sauté pan, heat the oil and cook the onion until it begins to brown, about 7 minutes. Add the garlic, spices, wine, tomatoes, and artichokes and continue to simmer until the pan is nearly dry. Add salt to taste.

Pour the tomato-artichoke sauce carefully over the eggplant and potatoes. (The dish can be assembled to this point a day ahead of time and stored in the refrigerator overnight.)

Cover and cook on low for about 4 hours, or until a skewer inserted into the stew easily penetrates all the layers.

While the vegetables are cooking, make the custard topping. Combine the milk and flour in a blender and blend until smooth. Pour the mixture into a saucepan and cook over medium-high heat, stirring constantly, until the sauce thickens enough to thickly coat the back of a spoon. Gradually stir in the cheese, then turn off the heat and rapidly whisk in the egg yolks one at a time. Stir in a dash of nutmeg.

1 russet potato, peeled and sliced

1 eggplant, peeled and cut into $1/4$-inch-thick crosswise slices

1 cinnamon stick

5 whole cloves

6 black peppercorns

2 allspice berries

$1/4$ cup olive oil

1 large yellow onion, chopped

4 large cloves garlic, minced

$1/4$ cup dry red wine

3 large tomatoes, coarsely chopped

1 (14-ounce) can artichoke hearts, well drained and halved

Salt to taste

Carefully pour the custard over the vegetables, trying not to dislodge them. Cover and continue cooking for about 1 hour longer, or until the custard is set.

Turn off the slow cooker and let the moussaka sit for 15 to 20 minutes, then carefully spoon up individual portions into a pasta bowl.

Tip: I find that it helps to slice the dish into 4 to 6 portions right in the slow cooker insert with a sharp knife before removing the portions with a spoon. That way, each portion is a little tidier.

SUGGESTED BEVERAGE: I would love a good Greek wine. I would enjoy Kir-Yianni's Xinomavro. And if you can't find any, opt for a full-bodied red or any good dry rosé.

Custard Topping

4 cups milk

$1/4$ cup all-purpose flour

1 cup shredded Gruyère cheese

2 egg yolks

Freshly grated nutmeg

WILD MUSHROOM STEW ON NOODLES

⇜ Serves 4 ⇝

Wild mushrooms abound in the mountains of northern Greece, and like everywhere else in the world where wild mushrooms grow, they make their seasonal appearance in stewpots throughout the region. Much to the surprise of many nonresidents, pasta is very common in Greece, too.

Rinse the dried mushrooms, then soak them in a medium bowl in 2 to 3 cups of water for 30 minutes. Lift out the softened mushrooms, leaving any grit behind, and squeeze the excess liquid out of them.

In a large sauté pan, heat the olive oil and sauté the onions over medium-high heat until beginning to brown, 5 to 7 minutes. Add the wine and continue to cook for another 5 to 7 minutes, or until some of the wine evaporates.

Transfer the onions to the slow cooker insert. Add the mushrooms, cinnamon stick, crushed coriander seeds, and bay leaves, then sprinkle the flour over all and mix in. Add the water and stir to combine.

Cover and cook on low for about 8 hours, or until the sauce is thick and savory. Add plenty of salt to taste. Carefully stir in the yogurt just before serving.

Spoon over freshly cooked noodles, sprinkle with the chopped parsley, and serve.

SUGGESTED BEVERAGE: I'd probably choose either a Greek or a Côtes de Provence rosé, or a young, medium-bodied, fruity red wine with this one.

3 ounces dried wild mushrooms

$1/4$ cup olive oil

3 onions, cut in half and thinly sliced

2 cups dry red or white wine

1 cinnamon stick

1 teaspoon coriander seeds, crushed

2 bay leaves

2 tablespoons all-purpose flour

3 cups water

Salt to taste

$1/2$ cup Greek-style yogurt or sour cream

1 pound fettuccine or linguine noodles, cooked just before serving

$1/4$ cup chopped fresh parsley

Yellow Split Pea and Oregano Purée

~ Serves 4 ~

As I have mentioned, lentils and split peas are big in the rustic cuisines of so many countries. Greece is no exception. This very simple dish can either be served on a plate by itself as an appetizer for dipping warm pita or as a side with grilled vegetables and a salad.

Thoroughly rinse the split peas and place them, along with the water, in the slow cooker insert.

In a sauté pan, heat the oil, add about half the onion, and sauté until beginning to brown, 6 to 8 minutes.

Add the sautéed onion to the split peas, cover, and cook on low for 6 to 8 hours, or until the peas are soft and foamy.

Fluff the split peas with a fork or use a handheld immersion blender to thoroughly blend the split peas, then add the oregano, vinegar, and salt to taste.

Allow the split peas to cool, and then spoon onto appetizer plates or one large platter. Sprinkle with the parsley and the remaining onion.

SUGGESTED BEVERAGE: A dry rosé is perfect here.

1 cup dried yellow split peas

6 cups water

1/2 cup olive oil

1 onion, finely chopped

2 teaspoons chopped fresh oregano

2 tablespoons red or white wine vinegar

Salt to taste

1/4 cup chopped fresh parsley, for garnish

Baby Limas with Spinach

⤷ Serves 6 to 8 ⤶

Here is another simple, delicious bean dish typical of what you might find in any Greek café. Be careful not to overcook the limas (unless you like them mushy), because they easily lose their shape with long cooking. The beauty of limas is that they have a very distinctive flavor and texture, both of which I adore. Serve the beans with a loaf of crusty country bread.

Rinse the beans thoroughly. Place the beans, water, onion, and garlic in the slow cooker insert. Cover and cook on low for 5 to 6 hours, or until the beans are tender but not falling apart.

When the beans are tender, stir in the spinach, olive oil, and lemon juice and add salt and pepper to taste.

Serve warm or cold.

SUGGESTED BEVERAGE: Again, if you can find it, why not try a Greek wine? Aghiorghitiko is a delicious red grape variety native to Nemea on the Greek mainland.

2 cups dried baby lima beans

6 cups water

$1/2$ onion, finely chopped

1 clove garlic, finely minced

$1/2$ pound fresh spinach leaves

$1/4$ cup olive oil

Juice of $1/2$ lemon

Salt and freshly ground black pepper to taste

The Middle East

Clearly, many Middle Eastern countries and cultures have a long tradition of soups and stews cooked for long periods in an oven or over an open fire, so there is no dearth of inspiration here for slow cooker adaptations.

The Lebanese Eggplant Stew is much like traditional Provençal ratatouille. Same vegetable repertoire, different seasonings. Harira is a Moroccan classic, usually made with lamb, and cooked for many hours during the Muslim month of fasting, Ramadan. For hundreds of years, its delicious smells must have filled homes with anticipation of that moment when the last rays of the sun disappear and devout Muslims can finally sit down at the table and dig in.

Although Armenia is not typically considered a Middle Eastern country, its heritage is much closer to that of ancient Persia than to most European countries, so I've chosen to include two rather unusual Armenian dishes in the collection. Khavits is close to American seven-grain breakfast cereals. So close, in fact, that you can use Cream of Wheat or a commercial seven-grain breakfast cereal for its base. The kicker is the topping of feta cheese, honey, and nuts. The Armenian Apricot Soup features one of our most popular stone fruits, which originated (like most of our stone fruits) in this region.

Hummus is a universal Mediterranean and Middle Eastern spread, and I have included a recipe for a sort of Egyptian "tostada," the Chickpea Fattet.

WINES WITH MIDDLE EASTERN FOOD

Pairing wines with the foods of the Middle East is an interesting proposition. On the one hand, you have a series of cultures and countries where grapes have been grown and wines made and consumed for several thousand years. On the other hand, you have the same cultures and countries from which the juice of fermented grapes has been all but banished since the time of the Prophet Muhammad in the seventh century.

Although the countries of the Middle Eastern region provided some of the first sites of serious wine production in the world (the pharaohs took wines with them to their tombs), wine culture today does not exist in most of them. This means that we are not likely to find traditional wine and food pairings in a Middle Eastern country. (The exception to the rule is Lebanon, a country with a significant Christian population, at one time referred to as the "Paris of the Middle East." Because of its pre–civil war affluence and its Christian population, Lebanon had a sophisticated level of wine appreciation and consumption. Today, fine wine production has met with a renaissance in this beautiful country.)

The good news is that the door is wide open, so to speak, and you have only your taste and your intuition to guide you in matters of food and wine pairing when exploring the foods of the Middle East. In the case of dishes that are strongly spiced, the rules for Indian cuisine might be useful: crisp, chilled whites, sparkling wines, cavas and champagne, rosés, and even younger, fruity reds. In the case of those dishes that are a bit more mild, such as the Chickpea Fattet made with hummus, I can easily envision enjoying a rosé, a red, or even a beer!

LEBANESE EGGPLANT STEW

⤛ Serves 4 to 6 ⤜

Many years ago as a student at the University of California, Berkeley, I was invited to a dinner given by professor Laura Nader, a Lebanese–American professor of Middle Eastern studies and sister of maverick politician Ralph Nader. Her dinner was simple and elegant, and the main course was a sort of Lebanese ratatouille. It was a delicious first for me, and contained many of the same elements as its French counterpart—eggplant, zucchini, tomatoes, and green pepper—but its seasonings, rather than being the basil and garlic of the French version, were more typical of the Middle East. You might serve the dish with rice and a simple salad of romaine lettuce, just as Professor Nader did so long ago. I would also offer some crusty bread on the side.

Combine the eggplant, zucchini, tomatoes, bell pepper, onion, and garlic in the slow cooker insert.

Using an electric coffee mill or a mortar and pestle, grind the peppercorns, allspice berries, cinnamon, and red pepper flakes to a powder.

Add the spices to the vegetables, cover, and cook on low for 3 to 4 hours, or until the vegetables are tender.

Stir in the olive oil and parsley, and add salt to taste just before serving.

SUGGESTED BEVERAGE: I think I'd choose a Merlot or Cabernet to accompany this dish.

1 eggplant, peeled and cut into 1-inch cubes

1 zucchini, cut into 1-inch pieces

3 tomatoes, cut into quarters

1 green bell pepper, stemmed, seeded, and cut into 1-inch pieces

1/2 onion, cut vertically into 8 pieces

3 cloves garlic, minced

1/2 teaspoon black peppercorns

1/2 teaspoon allspice berries

1-inch piece cinnamon

1/4 teaspoon red pepper flakes (optional)

1/4 cup olive oil

1/4 cup chopped fresh parsley

Salt to taste

CHICKPEA FATTET "TOSTADAS"

❧ Serves 4 ❧

Hummus is everywhere in Mediterranean cultures. In Greece, it is generally served as an appetizer, swimming in olive oil, accompanied by pita triangles, feta cheese, and olives. In the United States, it is also served as a dip for raw vegetables, and often has other ingredients, such as roasted red peppers or pine nuts, blended right in. The basic formula is pretty simple: chickpeas (garbanzo beans), tahini (sesame butter), lemon juice, salt, and olive oil. Proportions of the basic ingredients may be varied in accordance with your taste. Less garlic, more garlic, less tahini . . . whatever. Play around with it and see what you get. Fattet is a sort of Middle Eastern layered casserole or salad. Taking a left turn at traditional, it occurred to me that you could easily make a sort of Middle Eastern tostada using some of the common ingredients found in the dish.

To make the hummus, thoroughly rinse the chickpeas, then place them, along with the water, in the slow cooker insert.

Cover and cook on low for 6 to 8 hours, or until the chickpeas are tender. Drain the chickpeas, reserving $1/4$ cup of the cooking water. (You can reserve the rest of the cooking water for thickening soups or stews.) Measure out $1/2$ cup of the cooked chickpeas, coarsely chop them, and set them aside.

Place the whole chickpeas in the workbowl of a food processor. Press in the garlic, then add the lemon juice, tahini, olive oil, and 2 tablespoons of the cooking water and process until the mixture is smooth. Add the remaining 2 tablespoons cooking water only if needed to thin the consistency. Add salt to taste.

To make the fattet, in a toaster oven or under a broiler, toast the pita halves until lightly browned or crisp. Arrange the pita halves on individual plates, then spread each pita with about $1/3$ cup hummus. (Reserve the leftover hummus for another use). Sprinkle on 2 tablespoons of the

(continued)

Hummus

1 cup dried chickpeas

4 cups water

4 cloves garlic

$1/4$ cup fresh lemon juice

$1/4$ cup tahini

$1/4$ cup olive oil

Salt to taste

Fattet

2 whole pitas, split in half

$1^1/2$ cups Greek-style yogurt

1 teaspoon cumin seeds

1 cup chopped romaine lettuce

$1/4$ cup pine nuts, toasted

$1/4$ cup chopped fresh mint or cilantro leaves

chopped chickpeas, a generous dollop of yogurt, a pinch of cumin seed, $^1/_4$ cup lettuce, 1 tablespoon of toasted pine nuts, and 1 tablespoon of chopped mint.

Serve immediately.

Variations: Try adding artichoke hearts, kalamata olives, or roasted peppers when processing the hummus.

SUGGESTED BEVERAGE: If I were drinking wine with this, I would probably choose something light, aromatic, and white or something dry and rosy pink. That's *if* I were drinking wine with it. But "tostada" somehow makes me lust after a good beer.

HOT OR COLD LENTILS IN LEMON JUICE

∽ Serves 4 ∾

Here is another of those very simple, very refreshing, and delicious dishes using lentils. This is a Lebanese recipe, but it could just as easily come from Greece, Turkey, or anywhere in the Middle East. Serve warm or cold with pita, feta, and olives.

Rinse the lentils thoroughly, being sure to remove any small stones or dirt. Place the lentils in the slow cooker insert along with the water.

Cover and cook on low for about 2 hours, or until the lentils are tender but still hold their shape. (You want them slightly al dente.)

Drain the lentils and rinse them in cold water. Just before serving, add the garlic, olive oil, lemon juice, and salt to taste and mix thoroughly. Transfer to a serving bowl and garnish with the parsley.

Serve hot or cold.

SUGGESTED BEVERAGE: This is one of those dishes where I would enjoy a beer or even an icy-cold glass of Greek retsina.

1 cup dried lentils

4 cups water

4 cloves garlic, crushed

$^1/_3$ cup extra virgin olive oil

Juice of 2 lemons

Salt to taste

$^1/_2$ cup chopped fresh parsley, for garnish

ARMENIAN APRICOT SOUP

Serves 4 to 6

All right, Armenia can't really be considered "Middle East," but it is part of the botanically very important Trans-Causcasian region that begins in Iran. Botanically important because nearly all of our favorite stone fruits (cherries, peaches, apricots, etc.) had their beginnings in this region. This unusual soup combines the apricots of the region with lentils and vegetables. There are many variations and many ingredient possibilities, including bell peppers, tomatoes, mint, allspice, cinnamon, and paprika. In some versions, the lentils and vegetables are left whole; in others, they are puréed. Vary the soup to suit your taste.

Wash the lentils thoroughly, being sure to remove any small stones or dirt, and place them, along with the water, in the slow cooker insert. Add the onion, carrots, cumin, and apricots.

Cover and cook on low for 3 to 4 hours, or until the vegetables are tender. Add salt and pepper to taste.

If you wish, you can purée some or all of the soup, or leave it just as it is. In any case, garnish it with a dollop of the yogurt and a sprinkling of the mint.

SUGGESTED BEVERAGE: I think I would prefer a spicy, aromatic white wine, such as Gewürztraminer, well chilled, with this dish.

1 cup dried lentils

6 cups water

1 onion, chopped

2 carrots, diced

1 teaspoon ground cumin

1 cup dried apricots

Salt and freshly ground black pepper to taste

$1/2$ cup Greek-style yogurt or sour cream, for garnish

1 tablespoon chopped fresh mint, for garnish

THE MIDDLE EAST   109

ARMENIAN KHAVITS

~ Serves 3 to 4 ~

Although there appear to be many recipes for the Armenian dish called khavits, *most of which entail frying semolina or cracked wheat in butter before boiling it, the toppings are what hooked me when I had it for breakfast at an Armenian café in my town. You can crack your own wheat in a blender (see page 59), or use semolina, store-bought seven-grain cereal, or even Cream of Wheat. For added fiber, I usually include a couple of tablespoons of ground flaxseed in each serving.*

Place the cracked wheat, water, and salt in the slow cooker insert. (If you are using something other than wheat you have cracked yourself, use the liquid instructions on the package as your guide.)

Cover and cook on low overnight, about 8 hours.

In the morning, stir the cinnamon into the wheat, then spoon the cereal into individual bowls and top each portion with 1 tablespoon of honey, 1 tablespoon of feta cheese, 1 tablespoon of pistachios, and 1 or 2 teaspoons of flaxseed.

Pour half-and-half over the top and enjoy!

SUGGESTED BEVERAGE: I would opt for a cup of freshly brewed black tea, especially one that has fragrant hints of smoke, such as Scottish breakfast tea.

1 cup cracked wheat berries or seven-grain cereal

4 cups water (or according to package instructions)

$1/2$ teaspoon salt

1 teaspoon ground cinnamon

$1/4$ cup honey

$1/4$ cup feta cheese

$1/4$ cup crushed pistachios or walnuts or a mixture of the two

4 to 8 teaspoons ground flaxseed (optional)

$1/2$ cup half-and-half, low-fat milk, or soymilk

Chickpea Harira

~ Serves 6 to 8 ~

During the monthlong observance of Ramadan, devout Muslims are asked to go without eating anything substantial from sunup to sundown. Harira is a soup that is traditionally served to break the fast after sundown in Morocco. Although harira is most often prepared with lamb or chicken, a mighty savory version can also be prepared without meat.

Throughly rinse the chickpeas and place them in the slow cooker insert along with the water, tomatoes, celery leaves, and onion. Cover and cook on low for 6 to 8 hours, or until the chickpeas are tender.

In an electric coffee mill or a mortar and pestle, grind the cloves, cinnamon, peppercorns, cumin, saffron, and red pepper flakes to a powder. Add the ground turmeric.

Add the spices to the soup 1 to 2 hours before serving. (If you plan to be gone all day, you can add all the ingredients at the start. However, the spices will be just a bit more pungent if you hold off adding them until the chickpeas have cooked for a while.)

Just before serving, stir in the olive oil, parsley, cilantro, and lemon juice. Add salt to taste and serve, topping each serving with a dollop of yogurt.

SUGGESTED BEVERAGE: Consumption of alcohol is generally not encouraged by Muslim religious practices, so it's probably best to leave this one to your imagination or taste.

1 cup dried chickpeas

8 cups water

3 tomatoes, diced

1/4 cup chopped celery leaves

1 onion, finely diced

6 whole cloves

1-inch piece cinnamon stick

1/4 teaspoon black peppercorns

1 teaspoon cumin seeds

1/2 teaspoon saffron threads

1/4 teaspoon red pepper flakes

1/2 teaspoon ground turmeric

1/4 cup extra virgin olive oil

1/4 cup chopped fresh
    parsley leaves

1/4 cup chopped fresh
    cilantro leaves

2 tablespoons fresh lemon juice

Salt to taste

1/2 cup Greek-style yogurt

Index